THE WORLD IN ARMS

TimeFrame AD 1900-1925

THE UNITED STATES

THE MIDDLE EAST

EUROPE

TimeFrame AD 1900-1925

THE FAR EAST

Other Publications:
AMERICAN COUNTRY
VOYAGE THROUGH THE UNIVERSE
THE THIRD REICH
THE TIME-LIFE GARDENER'S GUIDE
MYSTERIES OF THE UNKNOWN
FIX IT YOURSELF
FITNESS, HEALTH & NUTRITION
SUCCESSFUL PARENTING
HEALTHY HOME COOKING
UNDERSTANDING COMPUTERS
LIBRARY OF NATIONS
THE ENCHANTED WORLD
THE KODAK LIBRARY OF CREATIVE PHOTOGRAPHY
GREAT MEALS IN MINUTES
THE CIVIL WAR
PLANET EARTH
COLLECTOR'S LIBRARY OF THE CIVIL WAR
THE EPIC OF FLIGHT
THE GOOD COOK
WORLD WAR II
HOME REPAIR AND IMPROVEMENT
THE OLD WEST

For information on and a full description of
any of the Time-Life Books series listed above,
please call 1-800-621-7026 or write:
Reader Information
Time-Life Customer Service
P.O. Box C-32068
Richmond, Virginia 23261-2068

This volume is one in a series that tells the story
of humankind. Other books in the series include:
The Age of God-Kings
Barbarian Tides
A Soaring Spirit
Empires Ascendant
Empires Besieged
The March of Islam
Fury of the Northmen
Light in the East
The Divine Campaigns
The Mongol Conquests
The Age of Calamity
Voyages of Discovery
Shadow of the Dictators

THE WORLD IN ARMS

TimeFrame AD 1900-1925

BY THE EDITORS OF TIME-LIFE BOOKS

TIME-LIFE BOOKS, ALEXANDRIA, VIRGINIA

Time-Life Books Inc.
is a wholly owned subsidiary of
TIME INCORPORATED

Editor-in-Chief: Jason McManus
Chairman and Chief Executive Officer:
J. Richard Munro
President and Chief Operating Officer:
N. J. Nicholas, Jr.
Editorial Director: Richard B. Stolley

THE TIME INC. BOOK COMPANY

President and Chief Executive Officer:
Kelso F. Sutton
President, Time Inc. Books Direct:
Christopher T. Linen

TIME-LIFE BOOKS INC.

EDITOR: George Constable
Executive Editor: Ellen Phillips
Director of Design: Louis Klein
Director of Editorial Resources:
Phyllis K. Wise
Editorial Board: Russell B. Adams, Jr.,
Dale M. Brown, Roberta Conlan,
Thomas H. Flaherty, Lee Hassig,
Jim Hicks, Donia Ann Steele,
Rosalind Stubenberg
Director of Photography and Research:
John Conrad Weiser

EUROPEAN EDITOR: Sue Joiner
Executive Editor: Gillian Moore
Design Director: Ed Skyner
Assistant Design Director: Mary Staples
Chief of Research: Vanessa Kramer
Chief Sub-Editor: Ilse Gray

PRESIDENT: John M. Fahey, Jr.
Senior Vice Presidents: Robert M.
DeSena, James L. Mercer, Paul R.
Stewart, Joseph J. Ward
Vice Presidents: Stephen L. Bair, Stephen
L. Goldstein, Juanita T. James, Andrew
P. Kaplan, Carol Kaplan, Susan J.
Maruyama, Robert H. Smith
Supervisor of Quality Control: James
King

PUBLISHER: Joseph J. Ward

Correspondents: Elisabeth Kraemer-Singh
(Bonn); Christina Lieberman (New York);
Maria Vincenza Aloisi (Paris); Ann
Natanson (Rome). Valuable assistance
was also provided by: Anne Heising
(Alexandria, Virginia); Elizabeth Brown
(New York); Dick Berry (Tokyo); Traudl
Lessing (Vienna).

TIME FRAME
(published in Britain as
TIME-LIFE HISTORY OF THE WORLD)
SERIES EDITOR: Tony Allan

Editorial Staff for *The World in Arms:*
Editor: Fergus Fleming
Designer: Mary Staples
Writer: Christopher Farman
Sub-Editor: Christine Noble
Design Assistant: Rachel Gibson
Editorial Assistant: Molly Sutherland
Picture Department: Patricia Murray
(administrator), Amanda Hindley (picture
coordinator)

Editorial Production
Chief: Maureen Kelly
Production Assistant: Samantha Hill
Editorial Department: Theresa John,
Debra Lelliott

U.S. EDITION

Assistant Editor: Barbara Fairchild
Quarmby
Copy Coordinator: Colette Stockum
Picture Coordinator: Robert H.
Wooldridge, Jr.

Editorial Operations
Copy Chief: Diane Ullius
Production: Celia Beattie
Library: Louise D. Forstall

Special Contributors: Stephen Downes,
Neil Fairbairn, Ellen Galford, Alan
Lothian, David Nicolle (text); Roy
Nanovic (index).

CONSULTANTS

General:
GEOFFREY PARKER, Professor of History, University of Illinois, Urbana-Champaign, Illinois

CHRISTOPHER BAYLY, Reader in Modern Indian History, St. Catharine's College, Cambridge University, Cambridge, England

Europe:
BRIAN BOND, Professor of Military History, King's College, University of London

Far East:
ANN WASWO, Lecturer in Modern Japanese History, St. Anthony's College, Oxford University, Oxford, England

United States:
HUGH BROGAN, Senior Lecturer in History, University of Essex, Colchester, England

Middle East:
MALCOLM YAPP, Professor of the Modern History of Western Asia, School of Oriental and African Studies, University of London

Russia:
ORLANDO FIGES, Assistant Lecturer in Modern European History, Trinity College, Cambridge University, Cambridge, England

Library of Congress Cataloging in Publication Data

The World in arms: AD 1900-1925 / by the editors of Time-Life Books.
    p.   cm.—(Time frame)
Includes bibliographical references.
ISBN 0-8094-6470-5.—ISBN 0-8094-6471-3
(lib. bdg.)
1. Military history, Modern—20th century
2. Revolutions—History—20th century
I. Time-Life Books. II. Series.
D431.W67 1989
909.82′1—dc20   89-20194
                            CIP

Time-Life Books Inc. offers a wide range of fine
recordings, including a *Rock 'n' Roll Era* series.
For subscription information, call 1-800-621-
7026 or write Time-Life Music, P.O. Box C-
32068, Richmond, Virginia 23261-2068.

CONTENTS

ECLIPSE OF THE OLD ORDER

As the world entered the twentieth century, it carried with it a host of dynasties who regarded their right to govern as a divine dispensation. The ruling classes believed that they were born to wield power, and political decision making, when not in the hands of autocrats, was delegated to administrations whose luminaries were still drawn mainly from the ranks of the hereditary landowning aristocracy.

In Europe especially, the status quo seemed well assured. Economies were booming as the result of rapid industrialization and colonial exploitation, and stability seemed guaranteed by a complex web of diplomatic alliances, reinforced in many cases by ties of blood or marriage: Kaiser Wilhelm II of Germany, Czar Nicholas II of Russia, and Britain's King George V, for example, were all cousins.

For the few, this peace and plenty allowed a life of extravagant leisure: Elegant gentry exchanged pleasantries and flaunted the latest fashions among the leafy surroundings of London's Hyde Park or Berlin's Unter den Linden; café society gossiped along the pavements of Vienna; revelers attended masked balls at the Paris Opera while duelists defended their honor in the Bois de Boulogne. And if the giddy whirl of the urban "season" began to pall, the country offered bracing alternatives: week-long house parties, race meetings, yachting regattas, hunting expeditions, and polo matches. The carefree prosperity of the time earned it—in later years—the name La Belle Époque.

Elsewhere, privilege reflected age-old tradition. For more than one-quarter of the world's population, the center of the universe lay—as it had done for centuries—within the 250 secluded acres of Beijing's Forbidden City, where 3,000 eunuchs waited on the occupant of China's Dragon Throne. And in the ancient city of Constantinople, a harem of hundreds cosseted the Ottoman sultan as their predecessors had done since the sixteenth century.

Below the surface, however, bitterness was growing among those unable to share this gilded life. In Europe, anarchist terrorists, intent on the abolition of all political systems and laws, assassinated seven heads of state between 1894 and 1913. And labor movements, clamoring for better working conditions, expressed their disaffection in frequent strikes. Farther east, the resentments grew into forces that were powerful enough to topple the old order. In the Middle East, the despotism of the Ottoman sultan was replaced by a constitutional government in 1908. In China, four years later, reformers who were seeking to revitalize the nation brought an end to centuries of imperial rule.

But the greatest change was to come with the Great War. For Europe's elite, the long, hot days of August 1914 were to prove an Indian summer; times would never again be so good. By 1919, following the carnage of four years of warfare, the Hapsburgs of Austria-Hungary, Germany's Hohenzollerns, and Russia's Romanovs—dynasties that had shaped the destiny of Europe for centuries—had been dethroned. The survivors among the patriotic masses who had marched so obediently into battle now emerged to reshape the world.

Franz Josef I, Hapsburg emperor of Austria and Hungary, was, at eighty-four, the oldest crowned head of Europe when he declared war on Serbia in 1914. The ensuing war saw Franz Josef's death, in 1916, and the downfall of his dynasty. Unable to hold on to the empire, his successor, Archduke Karl Franz Josef, abdicated in 1918. Archduke Karl died in exile four years later.

Kaiser Wilhelm II took his place as the third Hohenzollern emperor of Germany in 1888. A withered left arm did not dampen the strident militarism with which he led Germany into the world war. But with Germany's defeat, Wilhelm was forced to abdicate and take asylum in the Netherlands, where he died at the age of eighty-two.

By the time Sultan Mehmed VI ascended the
throne in 1918, the 600-
year-old Ottoman Empire
had become a constitu-
tional monarchy and the
sultanate had lost its autocratic powers. Mehmed
was forced to abdicate in
1922, shortly after the
foundation of the Turkish
Republic. He died in exile
at the Italian resort of San
Remo four years later.

Pu Yi was just two years old when he became emperor of China, upon the death of his aunt, the empress dowager, in 1908. By 1912, a nationalist revolution backed by the army had led to his abdication. Imprisoned and forced to embrace Communist ideology after World War II, the last of China's Manchu emperors died at the age of sixty-one, tending the gardens of his erstwhile palace.

THE GREAT WAR

1 June 28, 1914, was for most of Europe like any other fine summer Sunday, a time for enjoying rest and sunshine. General peace and unprecedented economic prosperity had lasted for more than thirty years and seemed set to continue indefinitely. There were a few problems, of course: Peace had not produced entire contentment, and wealth, though widespread, was far from universal. There were even a few pessimists who thought that a major European war was increasingly possible, especially since the Great Powers were divided into rival camps: The Triple Alliance linked Germany, Austria-Hungary, and Italy; the Triple Entente included France, Russia, and, tacitly, Britain. Both camps were heavily armed, and each had plans for a potential war against the other. But this was the twentieth century, a time of progress, not conflict. Almost no one foresaw how quickly a war could erupt, or how tragic it would be.

That Sunday, Archduke Francis Ferdinand, heir to the Austro-Hungarian throne and commander in chief of the Austrian army, was making an official visit to Sarajevo, the capital of his country's Balkan province of Bosnia. It was not a tactful gesture. Bosnia had recently been annexed by the Austrians, after decades of military occupation, and most of its Slav inhabitants felt some loyalty to the neighboring Slav state of Serbia. Bosnia seethed with embittered conspirators; that afternoon, one of them leaped onto the archduke's open car and shot both him and his wife.

Within weeks, these two deaths had led to hundreds of thousands more; within four years, to some 10 million. The action of a single Serbian was to unleash a horrific conflict that would touch almost every part of the globe, a war that was to enter the world's annals as the Great War. The victors would dub it the War of Civilization, an ironic title for four years of carnage in which the most advanced nations employed the full arsenal of technological progress to decimate one another's populations.

And with the slaughter came political change. Following a revolution in 1917, the vast expanses of imperial Russia emerged as the Union of Soviet Socialist Republics, the world's first Communist state. Germany lost its emperor and became, briefly, a republic. Rent by internal dissent, the Austro-Hungarian empire dissolved into its component parts. And in the Middle East, the once-mighty Ottoman Empire lay in fragments, its last sultan deposed by Kemal Atatürk, president of modern Turkey.

By 1925, a new order prevailed. The states spawned from the wreckage of the Austrian, German, and Russian empires gave concrete expression to nationalistic aspirations in eastern Europe and the Baltic. The rising sun of a frenetically industrialized and land-hungry Japan dominated the Far East. And in North America, the United States flexed its industrial and economic muscles as the new global leader.

The shots fired at Sarajevo were well calculated to cause havoc. Austria-Hungary was not a cohesive state; it was a ramshackle agglomeration of nations and fragments of

Austrian gunners on the eastern front during the Great War check the elevation of a 12-inch howitzer. The stubby weapon—named from the Czech word for "catapult"—hurled its massive shell along a high, lobbing trajectory that gave it fearful penetrating power against even a deeply entrenched enemy. Throughout the four years of the war, heavy artillery proved the key to success both in attack and in defense.

In early 1914, the balance of power in Europe set the Triple Alliance of Germany, Italy, and Austria-Hungary against the Triple Entente of Britain, France, and Russia. When Austria-Hungary declared war on Serbia on July 28, it drew all of Europe into conflict. Italy initially remained neutral but joined the Entente in 1915. By August 1916, the Central Powers, as they became known *(shaded orange)*, now comprising Germany, Austria-Hungary, the Ottoman Empire, and Bulgaria, were locked in combat with the rest of Europe. Only Sweden, Norway, Denmark, Holland, Switzerland, Spain, and Albania *(light brown)* remained neutral. The Central Powers made gains in the east, but their advance became bogged down in northern France *(inset)*, where the front line hardly moved until the months before Germany surrendered in November 1918.

nations, united only up to a point by dynastic loyalty to the Hapsburg emperors. In the lands that Francis Ferdinand would have inherited, power lay with two barely reconciled minorities, the Germans (mostly in Austria) and the Hungarians. But 47 percent of the population was made up of Slavs of various nationalities, and peripheral Italian- and Rumanian-speaking territories complicated matters still more. Vienna's rulers lived in constant fear that these subject peoples would break away from the empire, as the bulk of the Italian provinces had done in the previous century.

Therefore, when the Sarajevo conspirators were belatedly arrested and were found to possess Serbian army weapons, to have been trained in Serbia, and to have been smuggled across the border into Bosnia by Serbian officers, the outcry from Vienna was understandable. Not even Serbia's ally, Russia, could deny that the Austrians had a genuine grievance. It was the kind of crisis that European diplomacy should have

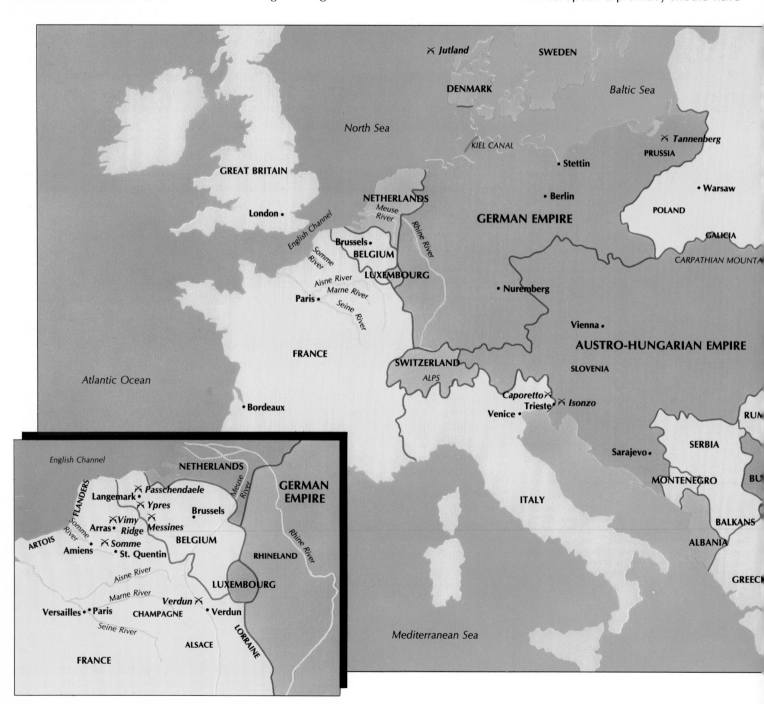

RUSSIAN EMPIRE

UKRAINE

Don River

CRIMEA

Black Sea

• Constantinople

Sea of Marmara

Dardanelles

OTTOMAN EMPIRE

ANATOLIA

been able to handle easily, and in normal circumstances, it would have.

But there were other factors involved that summer. By 1914, Austria-Hungary in its weakness had become almost a dependent of the Hapsburgs' mighty ally and protector, the German empire. A few months before the death of Francis Ferdinand, Germany had completed the Kiel Canal, which allowed its warships to move safely from the Baltic to the North Sea. Given the crisis, the canal had an ominous significance, for Germany suffered just as much as Austria-Hungary from insecurity.

True, Germany was rich and united, with thriving industries and the best educational system in the world. It was also the strongest military power in Europe, whose tightly disciplined and much vaunted army—which, when fully mobilized comprised some 2.2 million troops, including reservists—was constantly reinforced by a growing population. Yet these were not enough. Germany was a young nation, but an old culture. For 300 years before its unification under Prussian leadership in 1870, it had been weak, fragmented, and devoid of physically secure frontiers, the battleground of Europe. Despite the new state's strength, its leaders, and most of its people, still saw themselves as surrounded by dangerous enemies. Specifically, they feared the alliance between France and Russia, which carried with it the nightmarish possibility of a war on two fronts against superior forces.

The curious juxtaposition of strength and fear was not the only paradox at the heart of German policy. Although no nation in Europe desired peace, or realized its necessity, more than Germany, no nation was more dissatisfied with the status quo. Other European states had great colonial empires. The unification of Germany had come too late for it to acquire more than a handful of islands and a few sparsely populated regions in Africa. When German statesmen compared their colonies, not just with the British or French empires, but with the broad territories ruled by Holland, Belgium, or even Portugal, they felt deprived. To reflect the balance of power within Europe, a major reallocation would sooner or later be essential.

Changes were needed in Europe, too. For one thing, Germany's steel industry—then the key index of a nation's economic and military power—would shortly become dependent on imported ore. Native reserves, located in Silesia and Alsace-Lorraine, were running low. The richest reserves of iron in Europe lay just inside eastern France, but the French were not disposed to share them. Nor were lesser European states much attracted by the idea of the kind of German-dominated economic coordination that Germans thought essential to their national development.

There was one way to obtain these desirable changes. No German could forget that short, brilliantly planned wars such as the Franco-Prussian conflict of 1870 had been the means whereby their nation had been expanded and united, and Germany's rulers fully expected to use the same methods to bring the whole of Europe under German leadership. Despite Germany's yearning for peace, the nation was thoroughly prepared for war, and for its use as a means of gaining national advantage. Germany even had a plan that would avoid the two-front fighting it dreaded most.

Count Alfred von Schlieffen, head of the German General Staff until 1905, had analyzed the problem thus: In a war against France and Russia, the Germans must aim to overwhelm one enemy quickly before they were attacked by both. An attack on the Russians, whose enormous armies could withdraw into immense spaces, would never produce a quick, decisive victory. But the Russians themselves, hampered by poor communications, could not quickly stage an attack on Germany. It followed logically that the Germans must start the war by attacking France.

Since the French had fortified their eastern frontier between Luxembourg and Switzerland, on the German left, the attack would have to come from an overwhelmingly powerful right wing. It would crash through Belgium, outflanking the French defenses, then march westward, north of Paris, before wheeling left to encircle the city and take the French fortifications in the rear. After six weeks—the time Schlieffen deemed necessary to bring about a total collapse—the troops could be redeployed eastward by Germany's excellent railways, to deal with the Russians at leisure.

In fact, the Schlieffen Plan was less a solution to Germany's strategic dilemma than a military fantasy. It bore no relation to the old Prussian approach of limited campaigns and objectives, based on known means. Instead, a vast and paralyzing victory would be achieved by troops that in Schlieffen's time existed only on paper. Moreover, isolated from reality by the monastic seclusion of the elitist General Staff, Schlieffen ignored the moral outrage among other European powers that would follow from violations of neutrality—and the unavoidable military consequences of that outrage. His plan had a third glaring flaw. His advancing armies would have to march for weeks at a steady twenty miles a day deep into enemy territory and thus inevitably far outrun their rail-based supplies, while communications with Germany were dangerously vulnerable to any counterattack on the southern flank.

Nevertheless, Germany's leaders, among them Helmuth von Moltke, the nation's commander in 1914, rated Schlieffen as a great genius. When Schlieffen died that year, Germany's expanding population had in theory provided the troops the plan needed. The General Staff confidently awaited the opportunity to put it into effect.

And in Germany, the General Staff's influence stood high, because Germany's political system was as antique as its industry was modern. To the ministers and generals who governed in the name of the kaiser, the "all-highest warlord," the modern ideas of liberal democracy that prevailed farther west were inimical, and in Prussia, the heartland of the state, barely recognized.

Yet in the German parliament, limited though its powers were, the Social Democrat party, dedicated to gradual socialist reform, grew menacingly in strength, threatening the authoritarian system of German government. A national emergency, German leaders considered, might well bring dissenters back into the loyal fold.

War had almost come during a Balkan conflict in 1912, when the Austrians had pressed for a joint attack on Serbia. The kaiser and Moltke had been in favor, expecting a general war. But the German navy commander, Alfred von Tirpitz, insisted that his forces were not ready, and the decision was postponed pending completion of the Kiel Canal. Moltke wrote consolingly to his Austrian counterpart:

> A European war is bound to come sooner or later, and then it will, in the last resort, be a struggle between Teuton and Slav. It is the duty of all states who uphold the banner of German spiritual culture to prepare for this conflict. But the attack must come from the Slavs.

The outrage at Sarajevo seemed heaven-sent. In 1914, the situation was in some ways more favorable for Germany, and in others more urgent. With the canal open, the navy was as ready as it ever would be. The British government had been making accommodating gestures to Germany and might not stand by the other members of the Triple Entente; besides, Britain seemed on the verge of a civil war in Ireland, where nationalists were demanding home rule. On the other hand, Russia's railway

Pictured at a royal wedding in May 1913, Germany's Kaiser Wilhelm II *(far left)* and Britain's King George V *(left)* display public amity by each dressing in the uniform of the other's army. Although the two monarchs were first cousins, their respective nations were fierce industrial and naval rivals. By 1914, German steel production far outstripped that of Britain; nevertheless, the kaiser was still reluctant to fight a country that had poured its wealth into building the world's largest navy.

modernization was progressing at alarming speed. Accordingly, the German government urged Vienna to take a firm line with the Serbians.

After a month's delay, the Austrians presented Serbia with an intentionally brutal ultimatum, virtually demanding an end to Serbian independence. At the same time, the Germans insisted to the other European powers that the dispute was purely a private matter between Austria and Serbia, in which no outside mediation was possible. The Serbians, aware of the danger they were in, conceded every Austrian point but one: They refused to allow Austrian police and courts to operate on Serbian territory. It was enough. On July 28, 1914, the Austrians declared war on Serbia.

Perhaps, even at that late hour, a general European conflict might have been avoided. The Austrian declaration was simply a move in high-stakes diplomacy: Their army could mobilize only sluggishly, and no fighting was possible for weeks. The kaiser, whose bluster against his neighbors alternated with panic, might have drawn back from the brink if he had known how. But the Russian response to Austria's mobilization set in motion a war machine that was beyond its creators' power to halt.

Seeking to support their ally Serbia, while acting with moderation, the Russians tried to mobilize only a part of their army opposite the Austrian border, intending to leave the Germans unthreatened. But the complexities of partial mobilization were too much for their military organization. The czar could call out all his troops, or none. Reluctant to abandon Serbia, he ordered a general mobilization.

In Berlin, the dead hand of Schlieffen now ruled over German policy. If the Russians were given time to mobilize in peace, while the fighting was limited to Serbia, the master plan—the only plan—would certainly fail. However, it involved the immediate launching of a massive assault not on the offending Russians but on the French, who had so far in the crisis behaved with great restraint. Surely, the kaiser asked his staff, he could attack Russia only, and leave France alone? He could not. The kaiser bowed to the inevitable and the troops began to move.

On August 1, Germany declared war on Russia, and the German people, even the numerous Social Democrats who were in principle opposed to the kaiser's government and the capitalist state, flocked to defend the fatherland against the Slav barbarians. The first move in the great battle between "Teuton and Slav" was the occupation of neutral and defenseless Luxembourg. The second was left to the German ambassador in Brussels, who demanded that Belgium allow the kaiser's armies to march in "for reasons of self-preservation," unopposed by the Belgian forces. The Belgians, unable to see how this was compatible with their neutrality (which had been formally guaranteed by all major European powers including Germany), refused. On August 3, therefore, the Germans took their third step. They announced that the French had violated Belgian and even Dutch neutrality, had invaded the western province of Alsace, and had sent aircraft to bomb Nuremberg. In the face of such "provocations"—entirely imaginary—they could see no alternative but to declare war on France. Finally, on August 4, they invaded Belgium.

Thereafter events did not quite follow the German government's plans. True, the Social Democrats at home voted enthusiastically for war against both France and Russia, but abroad the kaiser's allies were less reliable. Austria-Hungary declared war on Russia on August 6, but the third member of the Triple Alliance slipped away. The Italians had promised to assist the Germans with a diversionary attack in the French Alps, and to send troops to fight in Alsace; now, however, they thought better of it. Other friendly countries, including Switzerland, Sweden, Bulgaria, and Rumania, had made less binding arrangements, and they all stayed neutral at this stage.

Far worse than the defection of doubtful allies was the enmity of Great Britain. Up to the last minute the German government had reasonable hopes that Britain would keep out of the war. There was a deep reluctance, inside and outside Prime Minister Herbert Asquith's Liberal government, for the country to become involved in what many scornfully described as a "Balkan quarrel," and even as late as August 2, Britain refused to consider itself definitely committed to an alliance with France or Russia. German diplomats desperately tried to convince London that they had no real hostile intentions. The invasion of neutral Belgium, in defiance of solemn treaties, decided matters. The British saw it as an outrage, and at midnight on August 4, united in idealistic indignation, they declared war.

Thus were the great nations of Europe committed to a conflict whose objectives were unclear to all, whose dimensions had been desired by none, and whose outcome was almost completely unpredictable. Yet the immediate reaction, almost everywhere, was wild enthusiasm. The cheering crowds in Berlin and Vienna had their counterparts in Paris and London, and internal squabbles were forgotten in a mood of exultant patriotism. Of course, almost everyone expected that the war, however terrible, would be short. The whole business would be over, so the common judgment went, by Christmas.

It very nearly was. The Schlieffen Plan almost worked, not least because the French did virtually everything possible to ensure its success. Victory, according to French commanders, would depend upon *l'attaque à l'outrance*—an all-out assault they were certain could come only from their 750,000 fully trained active troops, not from

Moments after his bullets killed Archduke Francis Ferdinand, heir to the Austro-Hungarian throne, Gavrilo Princip is seized by troops and police in the Bosnian town of Sarajevo. The assassin, a Serbian student, was one of a group of conspirators who saw the archduke's visit to Bosnia—recently annexed by the Austro-Hungarian empire—as an affront to their nation's honor. This isolated Balkan incident was soon transformed into a global conflict.

the 500,000 reservists spoiled by civilian life. Despite many intelligence reports to the contrary, they assumed that the Germans, too, would keep reservists out of the fighting line. As a result, although the French staff anticipated a German right hook through Belgium, they woefully underestimated its real strength. And their 1914 war plan supposed that one army, assisted by a small British expeditionary force, could block it, while the four armies of the main French force surged across the German frontier. Not even Schlieffen could have hoped for a more accommodating enemy.

French tactics in those first few weeks were as disastrous as French strategy. In the all-important attack, declared an official manual, "only two things are necessary: to know where the enemy is and to decide what to do. What the enemy intends is of no consequence." In Alsace, the flower of the French army paid a terrible price for this dogma, although the troops made a magnificent show. The infantry wore bright blue coats and scarlet trousers (the French despised the Germans' field-gray uniforms), and the cavalry was resplendent in gleaming breastplates. With blind courage, they charged the Germans; with mechanical precision, the German machine guns scythed them down. In two weeks, the French lost more than 300,000 men. By the end of August, the survivors had fallen back, dismayed, into French territory.

In the north, things seemed even worse for the French and British allies. From Belgium, 500,000 Germans ground their way into northern France, remorselessly forcing back the outnumbered French and the five divisions of the British Expeditionary Force. Although a series of short, delaying actions took a severe toll on the invaders, they seemed unstoppable: Day after day, the Allies retreated.

By late August, the Germans, tired but elated, were only a day or two's march from Paris, and the French government hurriedly left for Bordeaux. But no attack on the capital materialized. Instead, the Schlieffen Plan began to fall apart—partly because of the errors of the German commander—for just as the French had appeared determined to make Schlieffen's design succeed, so Moltke seemed equally resolved to make it fail. First, he had weakened his own right wing. A Russian attack was developing in East Prussia, earlier and far more successfully than German planners had imagined possible. In a moment of panic, Moltke sent four divisions meant for Belgium to the east, where they arrived too late to influence the fighting. Second, after the failure of the French attack in Alsace, Moltke ordered a counterblow by his left. The Germans succeeded in overrunning the much-desired French ore fields; but in Schlieffen's great design, the role of the German left was to act as a fixed hinge for the encircling right—not to try to drive the French backward out of the trap.

At least as important as Moltke's miscalculations, though, was the effect of the long advance on the German armies. They were near exhaustion, and their supplies were running low; even their boots were wearing out. They had suffered heavy casualties. They had no better idea than the French how to storm even rifle-defended positions without grievous loss, and a direct attack on Paris was probably beyond their strength. In any case, General Alexander von Kluck, commanding the German extreme right, had lost touch with the enemy in front of him. On September 1, he ordered his divisions to wheel south, east of Paris, hoping to outflank the French armies that had retreated to the Marne between the capital and the frontier fortress of Verdun.

Kluck's maneuver was not ordered by Moltke, who by now had only a vague idea where his armies were. Communications, as well as supplies, had almost broken down in the advance. The Germans had intended to rely on radio signals between headquarters, but the French had converted the Eiffel Tower into the first bastion of

LIFE IN THE TRENCHES

Scarring the soil of France and Belgium for 465 miles between Switzerland and the North Sea, the trenches of the western front rapidly developed from improvised foxholes scraped by exhausted armies in 1914 into a complex defensive system that was backed up by hospitals, supply dumps, and railways.

The trenches soon became a way of life for millions of soldiers. When troops such as the German unit shown above were not under bombardment or preparing for attack, they were engaged in a ceaseless routine of fatigue duty. Health as well as safety depended on spadework: Latrines and warm dugouts were as necessary as buried telephone lines and raised firing steps for sniping. The fighting men of both sides had to learn a range of new skills: the constant upkeep of barbed-wire barriers in the no man's land between the lines, for example, or the dangerous art of tunneling mines under enemy positions.

Yet life was not all misery: Most men, most of the time, were well fed. And a strange camaraderie existed between the combatants: Signals might be displayed to tell opposing snipers how they had "scored"; the occasional impromptu truce allowed each side to collect wounded and repair defenses; and one Christmas, opposing German and British forces ceased firing to play soccer.

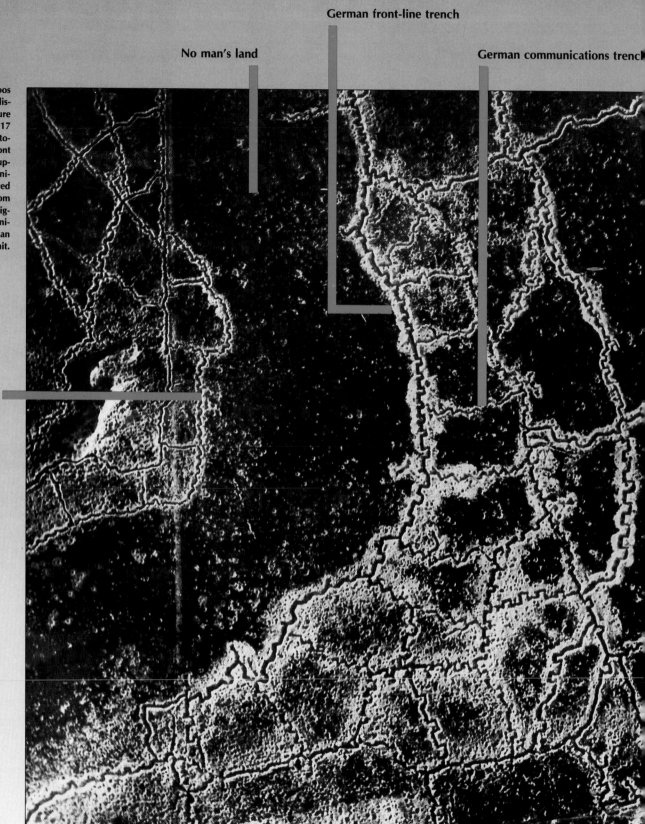

German front-line trench

No man's land

German communications trench

The chalky subsoil of Loos in northeast France displays an intricate structure of trench lines in a 1917 reconnaissance photograph. Between each front line and its rearward supports, a maze of communications trenches allowed troops to move, safe from small-arms fire; the zigzagging traverses minimized the effects of an artillery hit.

British front-line trench

Shouldering tools, a British fatigue party trudges to work on the Somme front in November 1916. Trench warfare demanded constant hard labor, especially in winter, and the weather could inflict worse misery than the enemy: Men often stood knee-deep, sometimes waist-deep, in water, with no hope of drying out until their stints were over.

Keeping his head cautiously below ground level, a British infantryman prepares to defend a captured trench during the Somme offensive of July 1916. Former enemy positions were dangerous places for their new owners to linger: In the likely event of a quick counterattack, the trenches' carefully built firing steps faced in the wrong direction.

A French soldier gives a fellow trench inmate a haircut in the Champagne region in 1916. A close-cropped skull was an important sanitary precaution against lice, which transmitted the debilitating "trench fever." Most people were infested after a day or two in the line, and a call at a delousing station was a priority.

Inspiring would-be volunteers, a British Saint George slays a Teutonic dragon in the 1915 recruiting poster shown below. The same symbol (*right*) served a 1917 German campaign to sell war bonds—although this time the knight carries a German eagle banner and spears an Allied monster. Posters—often the work of the best European and American artists—were an essential home-front weapon for every warring nation. Like the two shown here, they were used for recruitment as well as for fund-raising; they also served to whip up and maintain hatred for an enemy, or even, in blockaded Germany, to cajole women into giving up their cherished long hair to provide factories with driving belts for their machine tools.

electronic warfare and were jamming the airwaves. In Germany, it was known only that the kaiser's triumphant armies had crossed the Marne and were still advancing.

Smelling imminent victory, Chancellor Theobald von Bethmann Hollweg composed a memorandum setting out a possible peace settlement: a crippling war indemnity to be paid by France, great swaths of territory to be given to Germany. But before the chancellor formally proposed his terms, the military situation changed dramatically. French aircraft had spotted Kluck's swing away from Paris, and commander in chief Joseph Joffre had already prepared a counterstroke. While the Germans advanced to the Marne, the French rapidly improvised a new army around Paris. On September 6, as Kluck's troops swung past the capital, the French fell upon their flank and rear. (In an episode that became legendary, several thousand infantry

were rushed into battle in commandeered Paris taxis.) At the same time, south of the Marne, French armies that had been in exhausted retreat for weeks stopped, turned, and attacked their pursuers with an enthusiasm that astonished the Germans.

For five days the German armies fought on, despite their lack of supplies. But on September 10, one day short of the six weeks that Schlieffen had allowed for beating the French, Moltke ordered a general retreat northward to the heights beyond the Aisne River. The chance of a quick German victory—and a short war—had vanished.

Ironically, the Russian threat to the east that had so unnerved Moltke was already dissipated. The invasion of East Prussia, after initial success, had met with spectacular disaster at the Battle of Tannenberg. The Russians had acted with commendable speed in aid of France, but their staff planning was almost nonexistent. Without maps or effective reconnaissance, they launched two separate armies into a region of roadless forests and marshy lakes; unable to support each other, they were destroyed piecemeal by far smaller German forces. General Paul von Hindenburg, the German commander, became a hero to the nation; the army reserved its laurels for his talented chief of staff, General Erich Ludendorff.

Against the Austro-Hungarians, though, the Russians fared better. On the Austrian border in Galicia, the opposing armies collided with the enormous casualties that were becoming grimly commonplace; by September, the Austro-Hungarian forces were falling back in some disorder to the Carpathian Mountains. The Austrians received no consolation from their own assault on Serbia: The outnumbered Serbians fought desperately, and at one point even forced their way into Austrian Slovenia.

The strain of high command was too much for Moltke, who suffered a nervous breakdown. But his replacement, General Erich von Falkenhayn, considered the situation far from hopeless. Hindenburg was reinforced and launched a daring thrust into Russian Poland that nearly took Warsaw. In France, the German armies on the Aisne repelled Joffre's assaults with relative ease, and the fighting in the west developed into a race to the sea in which each side hurried coastward in an attempt to outflank the other. By October, continuous lines of battle ran from the Swiss frontier to the coast beyond Ypres, a historic town situated just across the French border in the west Belgian province of Flanders.

Both sides were short of troops and ammunition. Nevertheless, Falkenhayn launched one more major assault against the French and British at Ypres in late October, hoping to break through and capture the Channel ports. Into a narrow and vigorously defended front he threw the last available reserves: raw divisions formed from the volunteers who had enlisted in the patriotic fervor of August. Many were students, the cream of Germany's youth. At Langemarck they marched arm in arm, singing, against machine guns and regular British riflemen trained to fire fifteen aimed rounds a minute. The Germans called it *Kindermord*—or "child murder," the Massacre of the Innocents. The sacrifice availed little. Despite the near destruction of what remained of the prewar British army, there was no breakthrough. As the wearied survivors scrabbled trenches in the earth, the western front solidified along its length. And although the eastern fighting remained more open—another Austro-Hungarian invasion of Serbia was expelled in December—winter brought stalemate there also.

The war, however, was expanding: In October, the Ottoman Empire threw in its lot with the Central Powers, as the truncated Triple Alliance was now calling itself, sending an expedition into the Russian Caucasus. A small Ottoman force even threatened the Suez Canal, Britain's vital link with its eastern empire, tying down

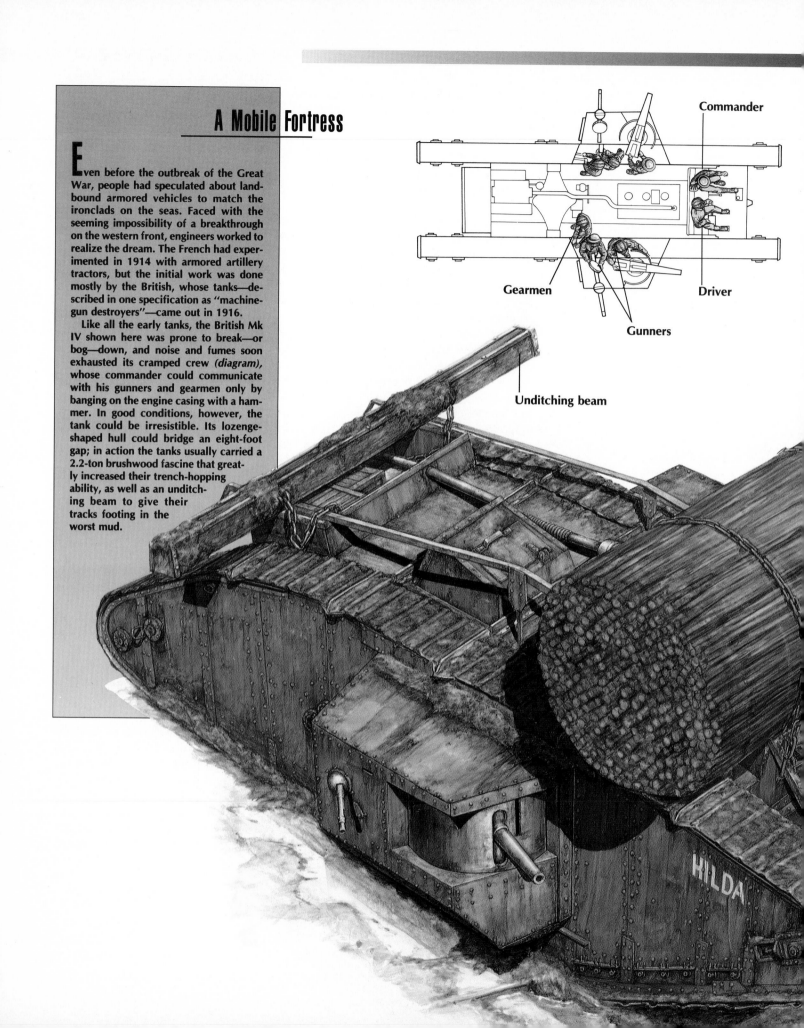

A Mobile Fortress

Even before the outbreak of the Great War, people had speculated about land-bound armored vehicles to match the ironclads on the seas. Faced with the seeming impossibility of a breakthrough on the western front, engineers worked to realize the dream. The French had experimented in 1914 with armored artillery tractors, but the initial work was done mostly by the British, whose tanks—described in one specification as "machine-gun destroyers"—came out in 1916.

Like all the early tanks, the British Mk IV shown here was prone to break—or bog—down, and noise and fumes soon exhausted its cramped crew *(diagram)*, whose commander could communicate with his gunners and gearmen only by banging on the engine casing with a hammer. In good conditions, however, the tank could be irresistible. Its lozenge-shaped hull could bridge an eight-foot gap; in action the tanks usually carried a 2.2-ton brushwood fascine that greatly increased their trench-hopping ability, as well as an unditching beam to give their tracks footing in the worst mud.

Commander

Gearmen

Gunners

Driver

Unditching beam

HILDA

Fascine

approximately 70,000 troops from Great Britain and the British Dominions.

Still, the Allies could take some comfort from the war at sea, where British power was scarcely challenged. Britain's Grand Fleet and Germany's High Seas Fleet faced each other tensely across the North Sea, but they risked only inconsequential raids. Farther afield, the German China squadron, deprived of its base when Britain's ally Japan joined the fighting, annihilated a few obsolete British warships off the coast of South America before meeting the same fate itself at the hands of the British a few weeks later. A handful of German commerce raiders managed to cause a good deal of damage and embarrassment before they were hunted down, but by the end of the year, the oceans of the world were virtually British lakes, on which Allied commerce sailed undisturbed. Just as important, a distant blockade of the Central Powers denied them access to many strategic materials.

As 1915 began, the belligerents took painful stock. Five months of fighting had brought unprecedented casualties: The French had lost 900,000 troops, the Germans 750,000, and the Russians and Austro-Hungarians had suffered equally heavily. Nonetheless, the enthusiasm of August was in every country replaced not by despair but by a determination to see things through. No nation would attack quite so recklessly again. But all still hoped for victory; the very number of the dead brought a general resolve that they should not have died in vain, and all the major powers began to reorganize their economies for a long war.

Manpower shortages were chronic: Prewar planners had intended their huge armies of reservists for a few weeks' campaigning, not an interminable struggle. Yet industry everywhere needed all the workers it could get, because the demand for munitions was vastly in excess of peacetime estimates, and all countries had difficulties in satisfying it. Wherever possible, women took men's places both at the workbench and in the fields, a move toward economic independence that would have profound consequences as the century progressed.

The Central Powers had the extra handicap of the British blockade, which was critically important in stopping imports of Chilean nitrates, hitherto essential in explosives manufacture. That particular problem was solved by the great German-Jewish chemist Fritz Haber in 1915, when he developed a process that ultimately allowed nitrates to be obtained from atmospheric nitrogen. Nevertheless, the list of blockade-induced shortages would grow steadily longer.

The Allies, too, had their special problems. The French had lost most of their coal and iron mines in the German invasion and were dependent on Britain for supplies. The British effort was hampered by almost complete unpreparedness: Britain's vast empire had always been run on a military shoestring, and alone among the major belligerents, Britain had neither a large conscript army nor the trained reserves and arms stockpiles that went with it.

Even in wartime, the Liberal government was reluctant to introduce compulsory military service. Instead, the war minister, Lord Horatio Kitchener, hero of colonial wars in Sudan and South Africa, called for volunteers. Somewhat to the general's surprise, young men flocked to his recruiting stations by the hundreds of thousands, in far greater numbers than could readily be trained and equipped, especially since most of the prewar regulars who would have to train them were either fighting desperately in France or already dead.

The Russian war effort was never short of men, and frantic industrialization brought Russia close to Western levels of munitions manufacture. But the Russian transport

An Undersea Predator

Dreaded by every merchant skipper, the submarine proved one of the war's most devastating new weapons. Its pressurized hull, able to withstand depths of up to 300 feet, was crammed with machinery: diesel and electric motors, batteries, pumps, and the deadly torpedoes. Compressed air forced seawater from its external ballast tanks *(below)*, allowing it to rise to the surface; when the pressure was released, the submarine sank beneath the waves.

In the midst of the submarine's pipes and ductwork lived a crew of more than thirty men who willingly accepted appalling discomfort for the chance to strike at their enemy. In 1917, German submariners came close to sweeping Britain's merchant navy from the seas. But the U-boats had their enemies, too. Hydrophones on surface escorts picked up the underwater rumbles from their motors, then depth charges shattered their hulls or forced them down till the ocean's pressure crushed them.

Ballast tank   **Control room**

and distribution system was chaotic. Later in the war, Russian soldiers would go unarmed into battle hoping to pick up the rifles of the dead and wounded, while supply depots far from the front brimmed with unused matériel.

Wartime demand and wartime shortages provided a splendid opportunity for the one major power that remained neutral. The United States found a ready market for its produce, especially after President Woodrow Wilson reluctantly authorized credit to the belligerent nations.

A plentiful supply of arms and troops, however, was not by itself sufficient for victory. A way had to be found to use them decisively. In France, would-be attackers on either side faced near-insuperable difficulties; barbed wire, dugout shelters, machine guns, and artillery made for an almost impenetrable defense. It was always possible to break into the enemy lines by throwing enough shells and men at them; the real problem was to carry on the attack after the first one to two miles. Infantry, though at dreadful cost, could capture ground, but cavalry could no longer survive on the battlefield long enough to exploit the infantry's victories. Nor could artillery advance in support across the shell-torn wilderness created by the attack. So the defenders, pushed back toward their supplies and railheads, could always re-form far faster than a second attack could be organized to follow on the first. And unreinforced, the attackers were always vulnerable to a rapidly organized counterattack.

Yet the Allies, unless they wished the war to end with the Germans occupying Belgium and most of industrial France, had no choice but to attack. The 1914 fighting had left the front meandering for 500 miles through northeastern France, but for much of its length, terrain and communications made large-scale offensives difficult. The French—with help from the British, very much the junior partners until their armies were ready—concentrated their 1915 efforts on the northern provinces of Artois and Champagne, in the hopes of "pinching out" a westward bulge in the German line. Despite heavy casualties, however, they achieved only trivial advances.

Essentially, fighting on the western front had settled into a gigantic siege operation, with no scope for the battles of maneuver that senior officers on both sides craved. But it would take time for the generals to learn that simple fact. In 1915 and 1916, they paid for their lessons with their soldiers' lives.

For their part, the Central Powers remained largely on the defensive in the west and attacked in the east. There, the situation was different. The fighting lines, sometimes

The Winged Warrior

The pressures of war crammed decades of aircraft development into four short years, turning the frail reconnaissance machines of 1914 into high-powered, specialized planes whose tasks ranged from photography and artillery spotting to ground attack and strategic bombing.

Yet none of these operations were possible without command of the air, and pride of place went to the machines that could gain it: the fighting scouts. The Fokker triplanes flown by the German ace Baron Manfred von Richthofen and his colorful "Flying Circus" were held in high esteem. But the British Sopwith Camel, shown here, was equally successful: Tough and maneuverable, it downed more enemy aircraft than any other type. Whereas early pilots carried only a pistol, the Sopwith had machine guns mounted on the nose of the plane, their firing rate synchronized to avoid damaging the propeller blades through which they fired.

only fifty feet apart in France, were rarely closer than two miles in the east; and not even the Russians could find enough men to hold a continuous defensive front, or manage to supply them if they tried. A war of movement was always possible despite the atrocious roads and climate. In a series of great battles from February to October, the German and Austrian armies drove the Russians out of Poland, taking more than one million prisoners and killing or wounding as many more. But there was plenty of space for a Russian retreat, and Falkenhayn, convinced that a final decision could be reached only in the west, refused to transfer enough troops to allow Hindenburg and Ludendorff to exploit their successes.

Far from the western front, the Allies made one major effort to break the deadlock. The British hatched a scheme that would use sea power to knock the Ottoman Empire out of the war. If the Allied battleships that controlled the Mediterranean could force their way through the narrow strait of the Dardanelles into the Sea of Marmara, they could bombard Constantinople, overthrow the Ottoman government, and open a Black Sea route to Russia, thereby completing the encirclement of Germany.

Had the Dardanelles expedition been intelligently planned and ruthlessly carried out, much might have been accomplished. As it was, when the Allied troops landed on the Gallipoli Peninsula on the western shores of the Dardanelles in April 1915, they discovered that Ottoman machine guns and barbed wire were just as effective as their German-manned equivalents on the western front. When the Allies abandoned the offensive in January 1916, they had lost more than 250,000 troops.

Gallipoli produced an important side effect. Falkenhayn responded to the Allied focus on the Mediterranean

Torpedo port

Giant of the Sky

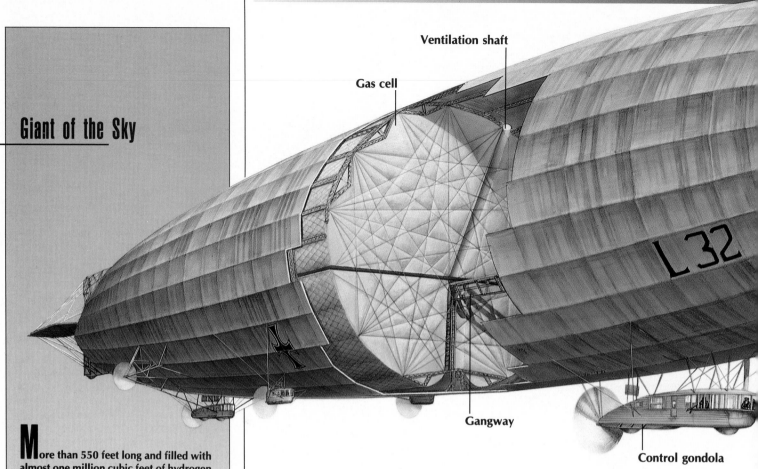

Ventilation shaft

Gas cell

L 32

Gangway

Control gondola

More than 550 feet long and filled with almost one million cubic feet of hydrogen gas, Germany's Zeppelin airships could travel higher, farther, and with a heavier load than any other flying machine in the war's early years. A crew of twenty or more included steersmen and engineers in the gondolas slung beneath the giant, as well as sailmakers who repaired damage to the linen-encased gas cells inside the aluminum framework of its hull.

In 1915, Zeppelins launched the world's first strategic bombing raids, on London and eastern England. Dropping more than two tons of bombs, they caused only modest damage but considerable alarm and consternation among the British people. An energetic defense, however, soon revealed that the Zeppelins were vulnerable to antiaircraft guns and the incendiary bullets of pursuing fighters: The hydrogen that gave them lift caught fire easily, and many crews were incinerated before airships were finally relegated to a scouting role.

by organizing an Austro-German attack on Serbia, aided by the Bulgarians. In turn, the French and British landed at Salonika in northeastern Greece, too late to rescue Serbia or stop the Germans from establishing a direct line of communications to the Ottoman Empire. But 300,000 Allied troops remained uselessly in Salonika for three years, straining relations with the supposedly neutral Greeks.

Meanwhile, the Triple Entente had acquired a fresh ally: Italy. Bribed with lavish promises of territory, the Italians declared war on Austria-Hungary in May 1915. But Italy was more of a burden than an asset. Britain had to supply it with coal and devote scarce shipping to its transport. It was not until the following year that the Italians could be induced to declare war on Germany, and in the meantime, the mountainous topography of the Austro-Italian border meant that Italian attacks—the next three years saw eleven of them, all along the Isonzo River near Trieste—faced appalling obstacles. But Italian participation in the conflict brought it, so Italian politicans reckoned, the status of a Great Power: well worth a few hundred thousand dead.

The first German attempt at a counterblockade of Britain, enforced by submarine, also came in 1915. Before the war, naval opinion had held that such a thing was impossible. Because submarines could neither carry enough sailors for prize crews to man captured ships nor find space to take prisoners aboard, they were held to be

useless against civilian vessels. In February 1915, the German government announced its solution to the problem: a declared war zone around the British Isles in which their U-boats would sink on sight any Allied merchant ship, crew and all.

The U-boats ambushed fifty ships between February and September. But some of the victims were passenger liners—and some of the passengers were U.S. citizens. When the biggest liner in the world, the *Lusitania,* was torpedoed off Ireland in 1915 with 128 Americans among the 1,198 dead, U.S. public opinion was outraged, and the Allies hoped that the United States would declare war on Germany. President Wilson was reluctant to take such a step, but the Germans were sufficiently fearful of the American reaction to call off their U-boat campaign. In any case, they were beginning to realize that they lacked the craft to make their blockade effective. However, plans for unrestricted submarine warfare were suspended, not abandoned, and German shipyards worked overtime building new models. Meanwhile, the British continued their own blockade. And since March, in retaliation for Germany's submarine policy, it had been total, including food.

The year 1915 had been another bloody and inconclusive one, and for 1916, Falkenhayn planned a different strategy. He attacked in France, with a new objective: not territory, but lives. The French would be forced into a killing ground of German choosing, where he would "bleed them white." He picked the old fortified area of Verdun, on the Meuse. Since 1914, it had stood in a salient, with no rail communications; yet the town, a centuries-old bastion of France's eastern defense, had a powerful symbolic importance, and the French would be compelled to defend it.

The French, outgunned and undersupplied, accepted the challenge, and their soldiers fell by the thousands in the shell-torn mud along the Meuse. But after early near-disaster, a stolid new commander, General Philippe Pétain, reorganized the defenders, contriving to supply a major battle by motor transport for the first time in the war. Gradually, the French assembled an artillery concentration that matched the Germans', and Falkenhayn belatedly discovered that attrition could work both ways.

As the slaughter progressed, the other Allies tried to relieve the French. That June, the Russian general Alexander Brusilov attacked the Austro-Hungarian sector, in the weakest part of the Central Powers' line. Whole divisions of the Hapsburgs' Slav troops surrendered without a fight to their Russian Slav cousins. Although some German reserves were rushed across Europe to plug the gaps, the attack at Verdun continued. By the end of June, the French situation was critical. German assault groups had advanced to within a few hundred yards of the last French defenses; and if Verdun fell after so much sacrifice, French morale might well collapse.

Only a Western counteroffensive could hope to draw off enough Germans to relieve the situation. The British had planned to attack together with the French along the Somme, to the northwest of Verdun, in mid-August, when their volunteer army would be better trained. Now, however, the attack was brought forward, and French support was greatly reduced. Still, the new British commander, Sir Douglas Haig, was confident that his amateur soldiers would break through. Joffre, less sanguine, hoped only that the British might inflict some more "attrition" on their joint enemies.

After a week-long preliminary bombardment, eighteen British infantry divisions—most of them in action for the first time—launched their assault on July 1. Tactics on some sectors were rudimentary: The troops, heavily laden with food and ammunition, climbed from their trenches at zero hour and plodded in regular lines toward the

German positions. But the 1.5 million shells the British had fired had only obliterated the surface features of the German line; the bombardment had even failed to cut much of the enemy's barbed wire. Most of the defenders, in dugouts sunk thirty feet deep in the chalky soil, were shaken but unharmed. Long before the British reached their objective, German machine gunners were in place on their ruined parapets. In a few hours, on the bloodiest day of the war, the British suffered nearly 60,000 casualties. Only on the southern sector, where more-flexible tactics were employed, was some limited advance achieved.

Still, Haig ordered his officers to continue attacking. Despite his casualties and the painfully slow advance of his troops (he never visited the front and had no conception of his men's difficulties), Haig did not lose faith in the possibilities of a decisive breakthrough. Even though the blunders of the first day were never quite repeated, five months of agony and an additional 350,000 casualties gained the British no more than five miles of ruined earth—although the Germans, with casualties of some 500,000, paid an even higher price for their dogged defense.

Meanwhile at Verdun, the French had found in General Robert Nivelle an artillery commander of great skill, whose cunning deployments surprised and misled the enemy. "Creeping barrages" of shells were planned, exploding curtains behind which the infantry could advance with some protection. By the end of October, most of the gains made by the Germans had been nullified.

Germany had failed decisively at sea, too. In late May, the High Seas Fleet had risked a major sortie, with the intention of luring out and destroying a small British squadron. Its messages were intercepted, however, and off the North Sea peninsula of Jutland, the Germans were confronted by the whole British fleet. In the action that followed, the Germans inflicted more damage than they received but, outnumbered, were driven back to port, where their ships would idle uselessly for the rest of the war.

By the end of 1916, attrition, painful as it was, seemed the only way to end the war—although it was hard to determine which side was dying faster. Quicker routes to victory were much desired, however, and innumerable technical innovations were tried. One of these, poison gas, sprang from the fertile mind of Fritz Haber and was used by the Germans in their only western attack of 1915, at the second battle of Ypres. (It had been tried on the Russian front, but Haber had not allowed for the astonishing cold that turned the gas to liquid and rendered it useless.) The effects were horrifyingly successful, but the German attack was not a large-scale operation. The Allies protested at Germany's breach of the codes of honorable warfare; nevertheless, they ordered their own chemists to work. Primitive gas masks were soon produced, and the soldiers of all armies learned to live with another horror.

Another invention, "land battle-

Sheepskin-clad against the Alpine chill, an Italian observation officer keeps watch on his Austrian enemies from a snowy outpost on Monte Nero above the Isonzo River near Trieste. During the Italian campaign, both sides struggled for the mountain crests, all-important for artillery spotting; and small groups of elite mountain troops fought one another in every kind of weather at altitudes of 10,000 feet. Usually, the ground favored defense: The Italians launched twelve murderous offensives along the Isonzo with little success.

ships"—the name "tank" was adopted to confuse enemy intelligence—came initially from the British Admiralty: armored, gun-carrying, tracked vehicles that could break through wire and cross trenches. A handful of prototypes became available at the end of 1915, and Haig hoped to have enough of them to lead his planned attack on the Somme. He was disappointed: Although a few took part in the later Somme battles, it was 1917 before a significant number were produced. Tanks had their drawbacks, being slow, mechanically unreliable, and vulnerable to light artillery. But their appearance frequently unnerved the Germans and heartened the Allies' own infantry. As the war progressed, the Allies relied increasingly upon them; the Germans, short of steel, never built many tanks.

Above the battlegrounds, new struggles began among the clouds. Aircraft, which before the war had seemed only sporting toys, were now serious instruments of battle. Air reconnaissance and artillery spotting quickly proved vital to every army, and by 1916, squadrons of fighter planes struggled for control of the sky. Unlike machine guns and poison gas, aircraft seemed to give scope for individual skill and courage, not mass-produced death and anonymous endurance. Successful pilots became national heroes, a status few lived to enjoy. Air-to-ground attack became a feature of every offensive, and bombing raids on enemy communications were common. The Germans pioneered attacks on enemy cities, hoping to damage civilian morale. Their giant airships, Zeppelins, began striking at London and other targets in 1915; later they were replaced by long-range bombers. Although the raids created initial panic and continued to inflict civilian casualties, their strategic effects were small.

Like Moltke before him, Falkenhayn had failed. As 1916 passed into winter, he was replaced by the team of Hindenburg and Ludendorff, fresh from further triumphs in the east, where the German riposte to Brusilov's offensive had cost the Russians another million troops. Under these iron-willed generals—Hindenburg the figurehead, Ludendorff the real power—Germany became, in effect, a military dictatorship. All men between fifteen and seventy were at the government's disposal, and factories were placed under army control. In a kind of moral coup d'état, the military, supposedly the servant of policy, became its master during the nation's crisis.

The Central Powers were perceptibly weakening. The blockade's effects had become serious, and even bread was scarce as what hungry Germans called the Turnip Winter began. Despite Belgian forced labor, manpower remained in short supply. The German army, after its ordeals at Verdun and the Somme, was no longer the matchless force it once had been, and Austro-Hungarian troops were reluctant to fight anyone—except perhaps the Italians, whom they despised.

The Allies were battered too, but they were not yet desperate. Britain, less badly mauled than France, prepared to take up the main burden: Prime Minister Asquith was replaced by a coalition led by the fiery David Lloyd George, conscription was at last in force, and new offensives were planned. Russia was the weak link, but in March 1917, revolutionary forces overthrew the ailing czarist regime. The Allies had high hopes that the new provisional government, led by the reformist Alexander Kerensky, would prosecute the war with greater efficiency.

The Russians would shortly be put to the test. Germany's 1917 strategy was a return to Falkenhayn's earlier prescription of attack in the east and defense in the west. Ludendorff—by now Germany's effective ruler—decided that the moment had come to play his trump card. In February, unrestricted submarine warfare was reintroduced,

A British sentry rings an improvised bell that serves as his unit's gas alarm. The man's 1916-model gas mask *(opposite)* was reasonably effective against chlorine, but less so against phosgene. Against mustard gas, no real defense was possible, since it penetrated most filters and raised suppurating blisters on exposed skin.

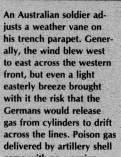

An Australian soldier adjusts a weather vane on his trench parapet. Generally, the wind blew west to east across the western front, but even a light easterly breeze brought with it the risk that the Germans would release gas from cylinders to drift across the lines. Poison gas delivered by artillery shell came with no warning.

CLOUDS OF DEATH

Silent and insidious, poison gas was more hated by those who had to endure its effects than any other weapon. Billowing from static cylinders or dispensed by field guns and mortars, as shown here, it filled trenches and dugouts, choking wounded or unconscious men where they lay and often causing panic among unharmed survivors.

The Germans, as world leaders in chemistry, were the first to experiment with gas, but the British and the French were close behind. Both sides began with chlorine, then advanced to phosgene and finally to the more potent mustard gas, an oily liquid whose vapor seared lungs, ruined eyes, and blistered skin. None were strictly intended as a killing agent: Their real purpose was to disorient and disorganize a trench's defenders, allowing an attacker an easy victory. Nevertheless, thousands of men died; thousands more were blinded; and others lingered in postwar sanatoriums, their lungs permanently damaged.

Yet gas was never decisive. Each side devised countermeasures—masks and so-called smoke helmets—that would allow its troops to stand and fight amid unbreathable air. With attackers and defenders similarly encumbered, the trench stalemate was unchanged. Only the general level of suffering had increased.

and this time neutrals, too, were sunk on sight. It was a great gamble: The Germans were aware that their U-boats would eventually bring the United States into the war on the Allied side, but they reckoned that they could starve Britain out first. Besides, if they could block the Atlantic, U.S. intervention would be meaningless.

The U-boats, at last available in quantity, did their work well. Between February and April—when a reluctant President Wilson finally declared war, though as an Associate Power, not a formal Ally—1,030 merchantmen were sunk; by May, Britain was reduced to four weeks' supply of some essentials, and the British Admiralty was near despair. In Berlin, hopes were high.

Meanwhile, the European slaughter continued undiminished. Most French generals believed that their own army was virtually finished as an offensive force. But Nivelle, Joffre's replacement as chief commander, managed to convince his dubious government that his artillery tactics were the long-sought key to victory. He prepared for a final April offensive along the Aisne that would blast clear through the German lines inside two days.

The Germans had plans of their own. From the Somme at the apex of their great threatened salient in France, they withdrew to the carefully prepared and much shorter Hindenburg line—a deep defensive zone of concrete fortifications, water obstacles, and barbed wire. Behind them, they left a zone of total devastation, with all buildings demolished, trees felled, and wells poisoned. On the southern flank of the salient, along the Aisne, they did not pull back but built defenses in depth.

Against all advice, Nivelle launched his attack anyway; it failed. By the standards of the war, it was a minor disaster, costing a mere 120,000 casualties. But Nivelle had

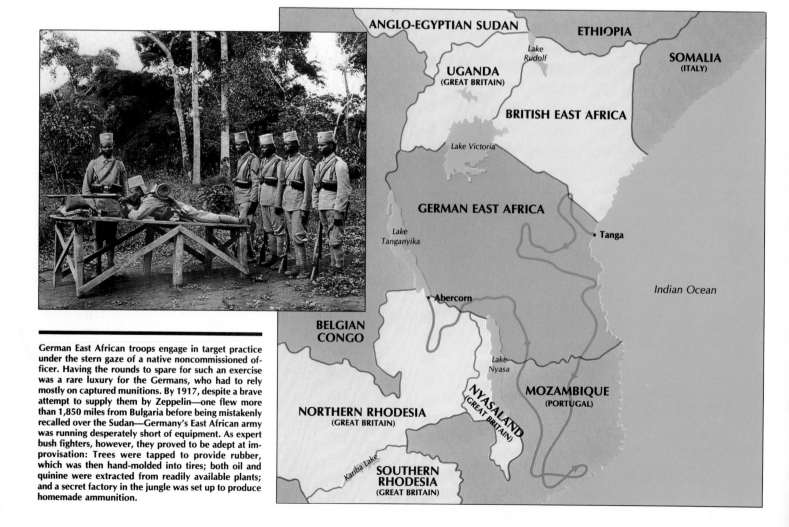

German East African troops engage in target practice under the stern gaze of a native noncommissioned officer. Having the rounds to spare for such an exercise was a rare luxury for the Germans, who had to rely mostly on captured munitions. By 1917, despite a brave attempt to supply them by Zeppelin—one flew more than 1,850 miles from Bulgaria before being mistakenly recalled over the Sudan—Germany's East African army was running desperately short of equipment. As expert bush fighters, however, they proved to be adept at improvisation: Trees were tapped to provide rubber, which was then hand-molded into tires; both oil and quinine were extracted from readily available plants; and a secret factory in the jungle was set up to produce homemade ammunition.

promised too much and raised too many hopes. The failure of his grand attack broke the heart of the long-suffering French army. The troops had simply had enough.

There had been signs of discontent in April, when some units marched to the line loudly bleating like sheep. In May, though, whole divisions refused to go into battle, and thousands of men deserted. Some regiments threatened to march on Paris or to destroy munitions factories, and a Russian division, sent to the western front as a friendly gesture, rebelled openly. By June, fifty-four divisions—half the French army—were in a state of mutiny, and at one point, there were no reliable troops between the Germans and Paris.

Remarkably, the French kept the mutiny secret and attempted to repair the damage. Pétain, who had served with distinction at Verdun, replaced Nivelle and remedied many of the army's grievances. There would be better rations, more leave, and above all, no more futile assaults; Pétain promised explicitly that he would wait for the tanks and the Americans before trying for victory. Some forty-six ringleaders were shot; the Russian mutineers were surrounded and destroyed by artillery. By the time the Germans heard of the mutiny, the French defense was solid once more.

Inevitably, the French near-collapse increased the load on their British allies. In the spring, at Arras and Vimy Ridge, and in the early summer at Messines, limited British offensives achieved their objectives. Their main attack, however, in late July, was aimed toward Passchendaele in Flanders. Haig had always seen the Flanders plain as the war's crucial theater. There, both Britain and Germany had their communications dangerously close to the front lines, and an advance of only five to ten miles could throw a retreating army into irretrievable disorder.

But the Germans could read a map as well as Haig, and their defenses were solid. In addition, the terrain was an attacker's nightmare: The clay soil was naturally glutinous, and years of shellfire had ruined its natural and man-made drainage systems. For months, Haig's despairing infantry floundered their lives away in the Flanders mud. Lloyd George made a halfhearted attempt to have the offensive called off, but Haig persisted: The British Admiralty, he pointed out, wanted the German submarine bases in Belgium seized before Britain collapsed from lack of supplies.

In fact, few German submarines operated out of Belgium, and when, three months and some 300,000 casualties later, the offensive was finally abandoned—it had "achieved its purpose," said Haig inscrutably—the British navy had begun to overcome the submarine threat.

Rationing at home had slightly eased Britain's supply problems, and at sea, hydrophones and depth charges were proving effective countermeasures. But the decisive factor was the introduction of escorted convoys for merchant ships, an idea imposed by Lloyd George on a reluctant Admiralty. Within weeks, ship losses declined dramatically and the threat of starvation was removed. Britain would survive, and America's transatlantic strength would make itself felt in Europe.

U.S. aid was urgently needed; both the British and the French were desperately short of men, conscripting troops they would never normally have thought fit for battle. And the Central Powers had triumphed over their other enemies.

Eleven battles on the Isonzo had brought the Italians no nearer Trieste; attacked by German units at Caporetto, they surrendered wholesale or fled in dismay. French and British troops were hurried to Italy in time to save Venice. But no reinforcements could save Russia. For a few months, the provisional government that had replaced the czar tried to keep the country in the war, and even won some victories against

The Bush War

Although most German colonies fell to the Allies within months of the war's outbreak, the situation was different in German East Africa. For two years, General Paul von Lettow-Vorbeck, with 3,000 European troops, some 11,000 native riflemen, and the 300-strong crew of the stranded cruiser Königsberg, beat back all attacks by the British, South Africans, and Belgians from their bases in neighboring British East Africa, Rhodesia, and the Congo.

When the South African general Jan Smuts finally took the port of Tanga on July 7, 1916, with a combined force of 120,000 men, it was the start of a tortuous chase across the African bush, in which Lettow-Vorbeck made masterful use of guerrilla tactics to outmaneuver and outfight the Allies. By November 1918, the Germans had invaded British East Africa, rampaged through Portuguese Mozambique, and seized a British settlement in Northern Rhodesia, before news of Germany's capitulation in Europe forced them to surrender. Ravaged by malaria and combat but unbowed, the force that finally laid down its arms at Abercorn on the southern shores of Lake Tanganyika comprised a mere 155 Europeans and 1,156 native troops. Never truly defeated in open battle, Lettow-Vorbeck had tied down approximately 130,000 Allied troops.

SHOULDERING THE BURDEN

As men by the millions volunteered or were conscripted for the fighting, their places in the farms and factories on which victory would depend were taken by women. The prospect of female labor in unfamiliar work produced striking, and to prewar eyes shocking, images, like the London lady pictured at left hauling coke. In most countries, war work was extolled to women as a patriotic virtue: The British poster below of a handsome and productive munitions worker, her long hair safely bound up beneath a working cap, was one of hundreds produced by the major combatant nations. But most women needed little urging: For the first time, they found themselves able to command high wages, as well as the independence that the money brought. And although at war's end many abandoned agriculture and industry, the place of women alongside men in the workplace was permanently established, and an irrevocable step forward in female emancipation had been taken.

ON HER THEIR LIVES DEPEND

WOMEN MUNITION WORKERS

Enrol at once

the Austrians. But the relentless German advance was a different matter. And the Germans had a powerful weapon inside Russia itself.

In April, they had allowed the Bolshevik leader, Vladimir Ilyich Ulyanov Lenin, to travel across Germany from his exile in Switzerland. In Russia, Lenin organized a second revolution, promising the people what they wanted: peace, bread, and land from the great estates. In November, he overthrew the provisional government and opened peace negotiations with the Germans. The German peace terms were rapacious; but since the Russian soldiers had gone home in search of the promised bread and land, the Bolsheviks had to accept them. By the Treaty of Brest Litovsk, concluded in March 1918, the Russians yielded Poland, the Ukraine, and the Baltic states of Latvia, Lithuania, and Estonia, as well as paying an enormous indemnity. Huge German forces were freed for service in the west.

In January 1918, President Wilson made a speech to the Senate, setting forth his Fourteen Points, an idealistic peace program that called for justice, not revenge, and a League of Nations that would guarantee security and the right of all peoples to self-determination. Britain and France, unconsulted, were distinctly uneasy: Both had large empires and both hoped for annexations after victory.

In Berlin, the Fourteen Points were scarcely considered, for with Russia out of the war, the Germans were certain of victory. The Allies could draw comfort from their brilliant campaign in Palestine that captured Jerusalem from the Ottomans, and from the knowledge that the Americans were on their way. But the Middle East was far from the center of the conflict, and even the elimination of the Ottoman Empire from the war would weaken Germany only slightly. The United States was farther away still, and it would be at least a year before its new armies made their power fully felt.

If the Germans, strengthened by their eastern armies, had remained on the defensive in France, the Allies would have found it almost impossible to drive them out. All the powers were exhausted, and Germany could have hoped for very favorable terms in a general peace settlement.

But moderation in this hour of triumph had no appeal to Ludendorff. Instead, he decided to play for higher stakes. In the east, not content with their existing conquests, the Germans pushed onward, infiltrating the Crimea and the Don basin and hoping to reach the Caucasus. And although their eastward expansion soaked up divisions that they could have used in the west, they determined to end the war in France with nothing less than total victory.

They even had some prospect of success, and not only because, for the first time since 1914, they had a numerical superiority over their opponents. The Germans had devised an entirely new tactical system, designed to get their troops through the opposing wire and deep into enemy lines. It was built on the novel idea of infantry assault groups—small, well-trained parties whose offensive power was based on the machine gun. These groups would attack immediately after artillery bombardments of unprecedented accuracy and intensity. When they met resistance, there would be no frontal assaults. The *Sturmtruppen,* or "storm troopers," as the Germans called their new, elite units, would always follow the path of least resistance, leaving enemy strongpoints to be dealt with later by follow-up units.

In March, the storm troopers struck. At Saint Quentin, on the Somme, the British front line dissolved before them. But as the shattered British withdrew across the old Somme battlefield, they had room to retreat without exposing any vital target. In five

Although Britain's worldwide empire remained remarkably loyal throughout the war, providing almost 40 percent of the military manpower at the nation's disposal, there was one violent exception. Predominantly Catholic Ireland, right on the imperial doorstep, had been close to civil war in 1914, when Protestants in the northern province of Ulster vigorously contested home-rule legislation passed by the British Parliament. But with the onset of war, the home-rule issue was postponed. Both sides temporarily buried their differences and between them sent 200,000 volunteers into the British army.

By 1916, however, one group of Irish nationalists could wait no longer for independence. Over Easter, the center of Dublin was briefly threatened by a rising of the Irish Citizen Army—pictured below armed with German rifles outside Liberty Hall, one of the few buildings they captured. Great Britain quickly crushed the rebellion with artillery and 12,000 troops, then ruthlessly executed its leaders. Alive, they had almost no popular support; as martyrs, they gave Ireland a new generation of heroes, and within three years, virtually the whole nation outside Ulster had become staunchly republican.

days the Germans advanced forty miles, an extraordinary distance by western-front standards, but they reached nothing worth taking. Then, with the arrival of Allied reserves, the German advance bogged down, and Ludendorff's efforts failed.

Still, the success exhilarated the Germans. The kaiser called it a triumph for autocracy over democracy. The Allies were correspondingly alarmed. Pétain in particular was near despair and spoke of abandoning the British on the Somme to save the rest of France. In this emergency, Haig asked for all the Western armies to be coordinated by France's General Ferdinand Foch. For the first time in the war, the Allies had something resembling a unified command.

Nevertheless, Ludendorff's second great blow, at Ypres in April, nearly broke through to the Channel ports. Although the British line bent, it did not break, and the Germans saw their casualty lists grow steadily. Their energies were not yet spent: Ludendorff, ever the opportunist, ordered probing attacks elsewhere to draw off the Allied reserves and found a weak spot in May when his troops burst across the Aisne and continued to the Marne, causing fresh alarm in Paris.

Thereafter, however, Ludendorff's offensives faltered. The storm troopers in the front of the attack had won victories, but despite the new tactics, their losses had been terrible, and the Germans could not replace them. Moreover, army morale was ebbing fast. The troops had been willing enough for one last great attack to end the war; now, realizing that it had failed, they yearned to end the fighting.

The French and British had lost at least as heavily, but they were now sure of American help: Although as yet only a few of their cobelligerents had reached the front, hundreds of thousands more were arriving every month. As the campaign continued into the summer, the German thrusts along the Marne were balanced by increasingly successful French counterattacks, for which hundreds of tanks appeared, along with a large number of American troops. June and July brought little additional gain. On August 8, which Ludendorff called "the black day of the German army," British and Australian tanks and infantry erupted from the mist at Amiens, and for the first time in the war, German discipline broke. Whole divisions fled from the battle.

The lapse was temporary, but the tide had turned. The Germans retreated steadily, pressed backward by the Allies in a series of battles almost as costly as those of 1916 or 1917. When the British drove through the Hindenburg line in late September, the last German defensive hope was gone. The Americans were by now fighting in strength, and throughout October, the German army fell back everywhere.

But at least the Germans held a coherent line in the west. Elsewhere, Germany's allies were disintegrating. An attack from Salonika in mid-September drove Bulgaria out of the war and threatened the Central Powers' whole southern flank. Austria-Hungary was in a state of internal dissolution, with food shortages and national groups declaring their independence, and a final Italian offensive in October overran an army that was already deserting in droves. A British attack from Palestine overwhelmed the Ottomans, who surrendered on October 30.

Faced by these debacles, the German leadership decided to call a halt. An armistice, declared Ludendorff, was essential. Hoping to take advantage of Wilson's Fourteen Points, the German government hastily demilitarized itself and put on the appearance of democracy. The kaiser abdicated and his successors sued for peace.

The German armies were incapable of much more resistance, but the final collapse came on the home front. The High Seas Fleet, ordered out for a death-or-glory attack on the British, mutinied. Disorder spread. Even before the armistice was signed on

A FLAWED SETTLEMENT

From January to June, 1919, world leaders gathered at the former French royal palace of Versailles, near Paris, to turn the armistice of the previous November into an enduring settlement. While German delegates waited in bitter impotence for the victors' decrees, ambassadors of the new nations already emerging from the ruined Ottoman and Austro-Hungarian empires sought recognition for their frontiers.

There was no doubt where the real decision-making power lay: with U.S. president Woodrow Wilson, French premier Georges Clemenceau, and British prime minister David Lloyd George. Yet there were acute differences among the three. Wilson sought an idealistic settlement based upon his Fourteen Points, promising peace in the world and self-determination for its peoples; Clemenceau—who remarked acerbically that "ten commandments were enough for God Almighty"—wanted a permanently crippled Germany; and Lloyd George, despite his personal inclinations to moderation, was committed to punitive terms that would win him a forthcoming election. The outcome was a flawed treaty that one American critic described as "the specifications for future revolutions and war."

Woodrow Wilson

Signed, sealed, and beribboned, the Treaty of Versailles bore the autographs of most of the world's leaders—the page shown below, taken from a copy retained by the French, carries those of the British and the Americans alone. The Germans deeply resented the treaty and publicly destroyed the master copy in 1940, after their armies had captured the French archives.

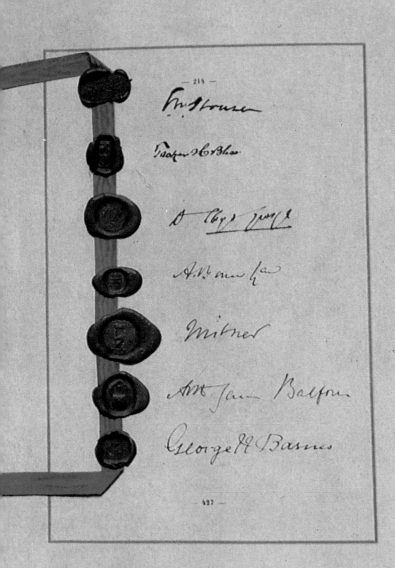

David Lloyd George

Georges Clemenceau

November 11, the kaiser had fled to neutral Holland, and a variety of provisional governments were proclaimed in a Germany that was only beginning to realize the magnitude of its defeat.

But the guns were silent. The Great War—it was only later that it became known as the First World War—was over. Civil wars followed within the territory of the defeated Central Powers and in Russia, where Allied forces, sent to keep Russia fighting the Germans, joined in against the troops of the new Bolshevik government. Nevertheless, the great clash of nations had ended. Early in 1919, the world's leaders assembled at Versailles to try to create a lasting peace.

It was no easy task. The victors could not agree among themselves, let alone with the defeated. To Georges Clemenceau, French prime minister since November 1917, Germany was the sole cause of the war and all its devastation. Its strength was far from broken: It remained a wild beast, waiting its chance to spring again. Victory had cruelly enfeebled France. The industrial northeast lay in ruins; and of the Frenchmen who at the start of the war had been between twenty and thirty-five, nearly half were dead or wounded. Clemenceau therefore demanded terms that would bind Germany hand and foot: huge financial reparations, complete disarmament, abrogation of the Treaty of Brest Litovsk, and French garrisons in the Rhineland.

Wilson thought otherwise. The United States had fought, not to save France, but "to redeem the world and make it fit for free men like ourselves to live in." He wanted

Following the Treaty of Versailles, the Central Powers lost only small tracts of land in the west, but the shape of eastern and central Europe changed dramatically. Greece and the new Republic of Turkey occupied the western tracts of the old Ottoman Empire *(shaded pale orange)*. Poland, which along with Latvia, Lithuania, Estonia, and Finland had broken free from the Russian Empire *(shaded pale yellow)*, now sliced divisively across prewar Germany *(orange)*. Within the borders of the Austro-Hungarian empire *(yellow)*, Austria and Hungary stood as independent states alongside Czechoslovakia; to the south, on the Adriatic, lay the new Kingdom of the Serbs, Croats, and Slovenes (now Yugoslavia); and to the east, Rumania had enlarged its territory at the expense of Russia and Austria-Hungary.

peace, not victory, and clung to his Fourteen Points. Such a program would inevitably dismantle the Austro-Hungarian empire and parts of the German; but, if carried out with generosity, it offered a chance of reconciling Germany to defeat.

Between these two statesmen, moving as advantage offered, was Lloyd George. As a practical man with experience in finance, he realized that there was no possibility of ruining Germany through reparations—it would be hard to extract money, and payment in goods would only upset the recipients' economies; as a politician with an election to win, he saw great possibilities in the slogan Make Germany Pay! But behind the scenes, he did much to reconcile Wilson and Clemenceau.

The Germans' view was very different. Their armies, they believed, had retired undefeated from the field and had already surrendered their lawful conquests in the east. Surely they were entitled to moderation in the west? Besides, they were negotiating under duress, since the British still maintained their crippling blockade.

Self-determination for eastern Europe was inevitable, given that most of the former subject nations had effectively liberated themselves as Hapsburg rule collapsed. The precise boundaries of the new states created at Versailles, though, owed little to Wilsonian idealism, because it was discovered that no borders could be drawn that did not leave national minorities on one side or other of the line. But there was no doubt who had won the war: Thus Italians, Czechs, Poles, and Rumanians found themselves ruling over German or Hungarian populations, irrespective of the latter's wishes. In the west, Alsace and Lorraine reverted to France. Overseas, German colonies passed, under League of Nations mandates, to the victors.

The Germans could countenance Austria-Hungary's misfortunes; their own territorial losses, however, were painful, and Clemenceau's proposed reparations were worse. (Even so, the French demands were very restrained compared with what the Germans had claimed at Brest Litovsk, or what the Germans had been planning to dictate after victory in 1918.) And the problem of reparations became entangled with another financial demand of almost equal magnitude—the repayment to the United States of loans made in the war.

The settlement eventually agreed upon was far less than Clemenceau had wanted—although he did get his Rhineland garrison. It had the strength of being underwritten by Wilson's League of Nations. But there was a snag. Just as Wilson had not consulted his cobelligerents before announcing his Fourteen Points, he failed to consult the U.S. Congress before creating the League of Nations. And Congress, tired of involvement in Europe's messy politics, refused to have anything to do with it.

The final outcome was almost the worst possible. Without American participation, the League of Nations, in effect, was a Franco-British committee. France, as Clemenceau had foreseen, was too weak to restrain an unfettered Germany; Britain was unwilling to help without American aid. The assessment of reparations was left for later discussion, and the wrangling continued resentfully for years. In the end, the reparations went largely unpaid, as did the American loans.

Thus the Treaty of Versailles neither crippled nor mollified Germany; and since it contained a clause denouncing Germany's guilt as the aggressor, it gave patriotic Germans an intense grievance. They had always believed the war had been forced on them; furthermore, they were convinced that but for unspecified treachery—"a stab in the back," as Ludendorff put it—they would have won it. Germany, though disarmed by the treaty, still had the most powerful economy in Europe. In twenty years, it would be ready once more to try to teach the world to give it due respect.

THE RUSSIAN REVOLUTION

At three o'clock in the afternoon on Sunday, August 2, 1914, His Imperial Majesty, Czar Nicholas II, entered the Saint George's Gallery of the Winter Palace, in the Russian capital of Saint Petersburg, and took his place by the temporary altar that had been set up in the middle of the vast room. The previous evening, Germany had declared war on Russia, and now the upper echelons of Russian society—the imperial court, the government, the aristocracy, the heads of the armed services—had gathered to join their ruler in praying for victory.

With the conclusion of the Mass, the czar repeated the oath of his predecessor, Alexander I, following Napoleon's ill-fated invasion of Russia in 1812: "I solemnly swear that I will never make peace so long as one of the enemy is on the soil of the fatherland." The reaction to the czar's pronouncement was recorded by Princess Cantacuzene, wife of one of the senior army officers: "Quite spontaneously, from five thousand throats broke forth the national anthem, which was not less beautiful because the voices were choked with emotion. Then cheer upon cheer came, till the walls rang with their echo!"

From the Saint George's Gallery, the royal couple moved onto a balcony overlooking the immense square in front of the Winter Palace. Here, thousands of ordinary Russians had congregated with flags, banners, icons, and portraits of the czar. As the object of their devotion appeared, the crowd knelt, flags dipped in salute, and launched into a fervent rendition of the national anthem. "To those thousands of men on their knees at that moment," wrote the French ambassador, Maurice Paléologue, "the czar was really the autocrat appointed of God, the military, political, and religious leader of his people, the absolute master of their bodies and souls."

But this outpouring of patriotic enthusiasm was deceptive. Beneath the facade of national unity, the country was deeply divided, with the great mass of the population bitterly resentful of the small, privileged elite surrounding the czar. Just nine years earlier, centuries of discontent had manifested itself in a violent revolution. The memory of its suppression, in which hundreds had been killed, lingered in the minds of many Russians. The hardships and horrors of war were to fan the flames of resentment. By 1918, the country would once again be in turmoil, with the monarchy overthrown, the czar and his family dead, and socialist revolutionaries vying for power. From that point, it would take three years of civil war before Russia finally emerged as the world's first Communist state, united under the leadership of Lenin.

The empire over which Nicholas ruled was vast, stretching some 8.5 million square miles from the Baltic to the Pacific and from the Arctic to the Black Sea. Over this area, much of which was empty waste, was spread a population of 130 million, of whom less than half were Great Russians, speaking Russian as their mother tongue.

Soldiers demonstrate in May 1917 in the Russian capital of Petrograd—known in prewar days as Saint Petersburg—beneath a banner demanding "land and freedom." Half-starved and decimated by the German army, the disgruntled Russian armed forces were an important element in the revolution of February 1917, which replaced Czar Nicholas II with a reformist provisional government. The change, the soldiers thought, would bring an end to the war, and by late 1917, some two million deserters had hastened to their villages spreading the message of peace and revolution. Not until the following year, however, after the radical Bolshevik party had seized power under Vladimir Ilyich Ulyanov Lenin, did the fighting cease.

The rest of the population was a turbulent mixture of fiercely nationalistic minorities—Ukrainians, Poles, Balts, Finns, Caucasians, Kazakhs, Uzbeks, Armenians, Tatars, Germans, Jews, and Mongols. Ruling such a vast and variegated population, most of them impoverished peasants, was not easy. As Nicholas's minister of finance, Count Sergey Witte, put it: "The outside world should not be surprised that we have an imperfect government, but that we have any government at all. With many nationalities, many languages, and a nation largely illiterate, the marvel is that the country can be held together even by autocratic means."

It was the overriding preoccupation of keeping the empire together that had marked czarist rule for the last 300 years. The main instrument of this policy was a class of dependent landowners who received and retained their estates in return for doing the royal bidding. As "service men" of the czars, they ruled over the countryside with absolute authority, leading the peasants into battle, levying from them the

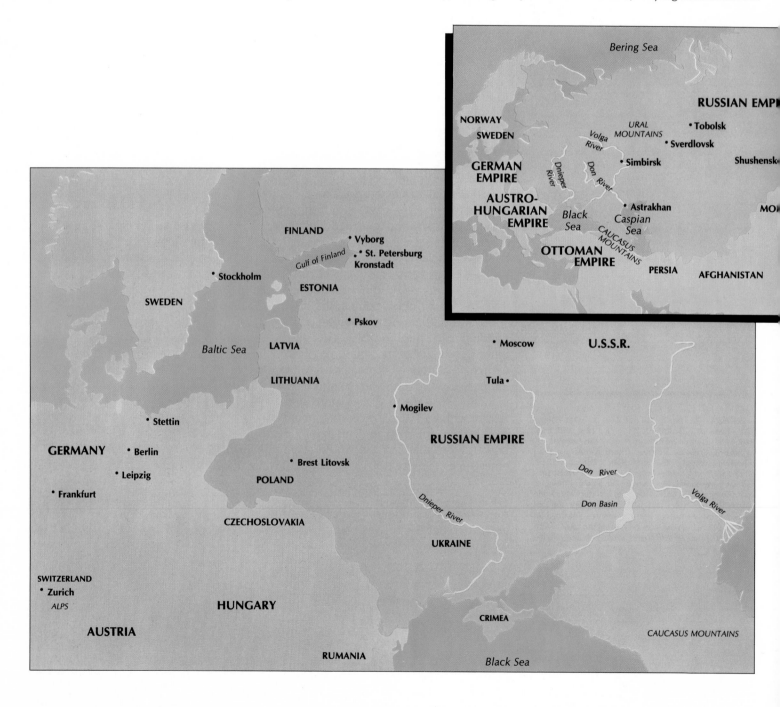

taxes required to wage war, and punishing those who refused either to pay or to fight.

In military terms, the system had proved highly successful, enabling generations of Russian rulers not only to consolidate but also to extend their territories. But the price of this success was paid in large part by the peasants, who had, over the years, been gradually reduced from the status of independent farmers to that of serfs, bound to the land and service of the local squire.

Starved, beaten, and despised, the Russian serfs were, in fact, close to being slaves. Divided into *miri,* or communes, they were subject to different laws from the rest of the population and were indeed considered to belong to a separate and lower caste of humanity. For many, the only solace was to be found in alcohol and a dogged pride in their closeness to the land. Some managed to throw off the yoke by escaping to one of the less settled eastern territories, where landlords and government representatives were as yet unestablished. Others expressed their discontent in various ways, stealing or destroying the crops of the landowners, setting fire to their barns, and killing such hated figures of authority as rent and tax collectors. In the eyes of members of the ruling class, the peasantry was a wild beast that had to be feared, chained, and kept under guard. And the knout, a braided leather whip six and a half feet long that could break a person's back with one blow, became a potent symbol of czarist power.

By the nineteenth century, the more enlightened and intellectual members of the nobility, especially those who had been educated abroad, had become increasingly dissatisfied with a system that kept the great majority of the Russian people in a state of medieval ignorance and poverty. In 1825, their discontent erupted in an anti-czarist coup led by liberal nobles and army officers. The revolt was quickly snuffed out, but it was the first signs of a conflict that was to dominate Russia through the nineteenth century and into the twentieth—that between the autocracy and the intelligentsia. Ultimately, however, it was to be a disastrous military campaign rather than any notions of enlightenment that signaled the need for change.

In 1853, Russia entered a catastrophic war with the French, British, and Ottomans in the Black Sea peninsula of the Crimea, during which thousands of peasants volunteered for military service on the false rumor that they would be emancipated. With Russia's defeat three years later, it became clear that the nation would have to modernize. Not only had the military leadership been incompetent and the ordnance inefficient, but many felt that Russia's primitive economic and social system had been a direct cause of defeat. In addition, the disappointed volunteers had taken to rioting on a large scale. Against a rising tide of popular frustration, Czar Alexander II decided that the best way of averting disaster was to introduce his own reform program, the centerpiece of which was the liberation of the serfs. As he pointed out to an anxious gathering of the Moscow nobility, "It is better to abolish serfdom from above than to wait for the time when it will begin to abolish itself from below."

In March 1861, notwithstanding monumental opposition from the landowners, Alexander signed the emancipation decree. The commune now served as a means of self-administration, whereby the peasants made collective decisions and allocated land. The trouble was that, as free citizens, the peasants received only half the land they had been cultivating as serfs, and they had to pay even for that. They were quick to show their displeasure: In the first four months following the emancipation, there were 647 incidents of peasant rioting; and during the year, there were 499 major disturbances that had to be put down by the military. At Bezdna, in the east-central province of Kazan, seventy rioting villagers were shot dead.

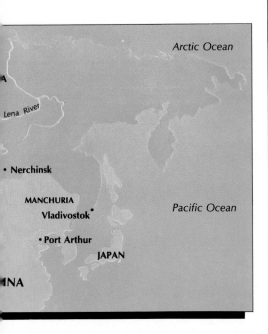

Imperial Russia, at the outbreak of the Great War in 1914, comprised 8.5 million square miles under the rule of one man: Czar Nicholas II. Within its western marches lay the grain-rich area of the Ukraine, as well as the once-sovereign states of Poland, Latvia, Lithuania, Estonia, and Finland. To the east, across the Ural Mountains, the vast wastes of Siberia stretched out to the port of Vladivostok. By 1918, following revolution and defeat, Russia had been deprived not only of Poland and the Baltic States but also of its monarch. The remnants of the czar's erstwhile domain became the Union of Soviet Socialist Republics in 1923.

The anger of the peasants was matched by that of the intellectuals, whose demands for legalized political parties and a freely elected parliament went far beyond anything the czar had in mind. Convinced that they would never achieve their objectives through peaceful means, many young dissidents turned, instead, to terrorism. Their prime target was Czar Alexander himself, who escaped no fewer than six assassination attempts. "What have these wretches got against me?" he asked after one near miss. "Why do they hunt me down like a wild beast?" The chase ended in March 1881, when two members of a terrorist group known as the People's Will succeeded in killing the czar with a bomb thrown under the royal coach. The reaction of the government was to rush through a series of draconian new measures—including strict censorship and increased police powers—which alienated even further the ordinary, law-abiding citizens without in any way deterring the revolutionaries.

By the early 1900s, the anticzarist movement was divided into two main parties—the Socialist Revolutionaries, or SRs, and the Social Democrats. To the SRs, it seemed clear that the only class capable of implementing radical social change was the peasantry, who made up 85 percent of the population and lived in an almost per-

Crowds throng the streets to watch the royal procession entering Moscow on May 25, 1896, the eve of Czar Nicholas II's coronation. Tradition dictated that the ancient ritual take place not in Saint Petersburg but in Moscow, the symbolic center of Russia and, until 1713, its capital. The grandeur of the five-hour coronation ceremony, held at Moscow's Cathedral of the Assumption and followed by a banquet for 7,000 people, was marred by tragedy. The following day, hundreds of people were killed in a stampede that erupted after a rumor spread that beer was in short supply at an open-air feast for the people of Moscow.

manent state of disaffection. Many SRs believed, moreover, that the traditional form of village organization, the commune, with its emphasis on common ownership and collective decision making, was a model for the socialist society of the future.

The Social Democrats dismissed such views as "populist" and "utopian," arguing that the struggle for socialism had to be carried on in accordance with "scientific" principles—which meant in accordance with the principles laid down by the German left-wing philosopher Karl Marx. Marx had died in London in 1883, after a long and penurious exile. But he had passed on to the world one important bequest: a theory that purported to explain the prime cause of historical change. In Marx's view, humankind progressed as a result of the conflict between classes, passing through three major stages on the road to political perfection: feudalism, capitalism, and socialism. The final stage, socialism, would come about when the workers, or proletariat, seized power from their capitalist oppressors and ushered in the first entirely classless—and harmonious—society.

It was the near-religious certainty underlying this theory of history that made Marxism so appealing to the revolutionaries. No matter how hard their struggle or how great their sacrifice, they found consolation in the conviction that time would bring victory. Even so, applying Marxist theory to Russian conditions called for a heroic degree of optimism. Marx's view was that socialism could be accomplished only by the proletariat. In Russia, however, where industrialization had just begun and the urban proletariat was tiny in comparison with the peasantry, capitalism was to all appearances in its infancy, and the conditions propounded by Marx as necessary for revolution seemed far away. Meanwhile, the Social Democrats had to get on with the vital if humdrum task of spreading the Marxist message. Their efforts soon bore fruit. According to a police report in 1901:

Nicholas II, his wife, Alexandra, and their children—the grand duchesses Tatiana, Marie, Anastasia, Olga, and the czarevitch Alexis—gather for a family portrait. Nicholas, who wrote that his accession was "the worst thing that could have happened to me," was an unwilling monarch. A shy man devoted to his wife, who herself shunned court society, he spent much of his time secluded at the summer palace of Tsarskoye Selo, outside Saint Petersburg. Knowing little of life in the rest of Russia and concerned mainly with his family, the czar was out of touch with courtier and commoner alike. It was an isolation that would eventually contribute to his downfall and the death of the family he loved.

Agitators . . . have achieved some success, unfortunately, in organizing the workers to fight against the government. Within the last three or four years, the easygoing Russian young man has been transformed into a special type of semiliterate "intelligent," who feels obliged to spurn family and religion, to disregard the law, and to deny and scoff at constituted authority. Fortunately such young men are not numerous in the factories, but this negligible handful terrorizes the inert majority of workers into following it.

The truth was that low wages, bad housing, and inhumane working conditions had given the proletariat as great a sense of grievance as that of the peasantry. The workers proved highly receptive, therefore, to the propaganda of the Social Democrats, and some among the party leadership began to look forward to the emergence of a mass labor movement similar to those in more liberal Western countries such as Britain and France. There were others, however, who believed that such a movement would lose

Under the Yoke

Life for the Russian peasantry at the turn of the century was harsh in the extreme. After their emancipation in 1861, the peasants were forced to pay for the land that they had previously farmed for the landowners. This, together with an increasing population, high rents, and frequent famines, meant that many were worse off than before. Sales taxes—especially that on liquor, the peasants' principal solace—were a crippling burden. By 1900, liquor tax was the largest single item of revenue in the imperial budget.

These high taxes were poured into a massive program of industrial development, and many peasants went to the new factories to earn a living, leaving the fields to be tilled by relatives until they could return home for the harvest. Urban conditions were dreadful—both factory and tenement were dangerous and unsanitary. The work day was eleven or twelve hours, and safety standards were virtually nonexistent. Even the reports of the government's factory inspectorate, set up in 1882, were so critical that they were withheld from publication.

Harnessed like beasts of burden, peasant women haul a barge along the Volga River in 1913. Russian peasants were considered by many landlords to be on the same level as animals. Conditions in the towns were no better than in the country; women made up 27 percent of the urban labor force, working the same hours as men, with no concessions even for pregnancy.

its revolutionary character and become a vehicle for reform rather than change. The fiercest critic of the "reformist" view was a young lawyer, Vladimir Ilyich Ulyanov—better known to his comrades as V. I. Lenin.

Born in 1870, in the small town of Simbirsk (now Ulyanovsk), on the Volga River, the son of well-to-do middle-class parents, Lenin had enjoyed a comfortable and carefree childhood. In 1887, however, when his elder brother, a student at Saint Petersburg University, was hanged for his part in an abortive plot to kill the czar, Lenin became a committed Marxist.

For the next thirteen years, he devoted himself to revolutionary activities, maintaining contact with fellow Marxists through a network of small, informal discussion

groups that often met in private houses. Though physically unprepossessing, with a balding head and a thin, reddish beard, he displayed a vigor, intelligence, and determination that distinguished him from his peers. After Lenin had visited Switzerland in 1895, to make contact with some of the Marxist luminaries living in exile, one of his hosts wrote, "I felt that I had before me a man who would be the leader of the Russian Revolution. He not only was a cultured Marxist—of these there were many—but he also knew what he wanted to do and how to do it."

Lenin produced a number of pamphlets and essays—the start of a literary avalanche that was to swell to some 10 million words before his death—and delivered lectures on Marx's most important work, *Das Kapital*. On a more direct level, he smuggled seditious literature into the country and forged links with the Saint Petersburg factory workers in preparation for future strikes.

Lenin seems to have enjoyed the role of political conspirator, with its elaborate ruses against the police and its paraphernalia of false names, hidden messages, and secret codes. His wife, Krupskaya, an equally committed Marxist, later recalled that of all the underground groups working in Saint Petersburg, his was the best at outwitting the authorities. "He knew all the through courtyards," she wrote. "He taught us how to write in books with invisible ink, or by the dot method; how to mark secret signs, and thought out all manner of aliases."

However cunning his methods, Lenin was not infallible. On December 8, 1895, acting on a tip-off from one of their agents inside the group, the police arrested him as he was preparing the first issue of a new socialist paper. The next

Workers from Petrograd's Putilov factory face the camera dejectedly in their cramped accommodations. Such rooms typically housed several families, each occupying a corner curtained off to provide a semblance of privacy.

four years of Siberian exile did little to dampen his ardor. Upon his release in 1900, he settled temporarily at Pskov near the Estonian border and immediately returned to the task that had been occupying him at the time of his arrest—the establishment of a revolutionary paper, *Iskra (The Spark),* that would serve as a rallying point for the scores of underground Social Democratic groups that were now flourishing throughout the country.

It was now that he first called himself Lenin, a name derived from the Lena, the longest river in Siberia. To avoid imprisonment by the Russian authorities, Lenin was forced to print his new paper in other European countries. Accordingly, with his new pseudonym he adopted a new life—that of the wandering political émigré. Krupskaya's reunion with him in Munich, early in 1901, signaled the start of a sixteen-year exile that was to take them through a succession of dreary backstreet boarding houses in half a dozen European cities.

During these years of travel, Lenin maintained close contacts with other revolutionaries in exile, and in the summer of 1901, he attended the Social Democrats' Second Congress, held in Brussels and London. It was an event that would lead to a fundamental rift within the party. By now, the Social Democrats were embroiled in the argument over "reformism," and delegates were faced with a crucial choice: to support Lenin's concept of an elite organization consisting of a few highly dedicated individuals, or to accept the idea espoused by his opponent, Yuly Martov, of a broadly based party open to anyone.

Much to Lenin's dismay, the Congress rejected his ideas, voting by a small majority to accept Martov's line on membership. On the other hand, Lenin and his supporters were victorious in the elections to the editorial board of *Iskra* and to the central committee. It was on the strength of these victories that the Leninists would henceforth call themselves Bolsheviks, or "men of the majority," and dub their opponents Mensheviks, or "men of the minority."

The roles were soon reversed, because by 1904, the *Iskra* board as well as the central committee had fallen into the hands of the Mensheviks. Unwilling to serve under his rivals, Lenin decided to resign from *Iskra* and to launch a new paper of his own, *Vperyod (Forward),* published in Geneva. One of his visitors described Lenin's attitude toward the Mensheviks at this time: When talking about his rivals, "he could hardly control himself. He would suddenly stop in the middle of the pavement, stick his fingers into the holes of his waistcoat . . . lean back, then jump forward, letting fly at his enemies. He cared nothing for the fact that passersby stared with some amazement at his gesticulations."

While divisions were appearing in the ranks of the Social Democrats, imperial Russia was grinding its way to outright collapse. In February 1904, a longstanding rivalry between Russia and Japan over territory in the Far East resulted in a surprise Japanese attack on Port Arthur, the Russian naval base in Manchuria. The ensuing war lasted only eighteen months, but in that time, Russia suffered a series of humiliating defeats that fanned the flames of political discontent. Strikes and demonstrations erupted in many parts of the country, and the terrorist wing of the SRs, who had meanwhile been increasing their support among the peasants, succeeded in assassinating a number of prominent figures, including the czar's favorite minister, Vyacheslav Plehve.

The more clear-sighted of the czar's advisers urged him to defuse the situation by introducing an immediate and far-reaching program of reform. But Czar Nicholas II

Inhabitants of Saint Petersburg crowd the pavements in October 1905, as workers march through the city bearing banners calling for an end to autocracy. In January of that year, following heavy Russian losses in the Russo-Japanese War, popular opposition to the government had erupted into revolution. Strikes swept the country as people of all classes and walks of life demanded an end to the czar's absolute rule. In October, with Saint Petersburg at a standstill and peasants seizing land in the countryside, the czar finally issued a document, the October Manifesto, providing for an elected assembly. Although the reforms did little to limit the czar's powers, they temporarily appeased the people and broke the revolutionary mood of the country.

was not the kind of ruler to be swayed by political considerations. Ascending the throne in 1894, aged twenty-six, he had pledged himself to "maintain the principle of autocracy just as firmly and unflinchingly as it was preserved by my unforgettable dead father" (Czar Alexander III)—and the past ten years had shown him to be as good as his word.

It was entirely in character, therefore, that Nicholas chose to ignore the appeal that was sent to him on January 21, 1905. Signed by a priest, Father Georgi Gapon, it urged him to receive, in person, a petition that the workers of Saint Petersburg intended to deliver to the Winter Palace the following afternoon. The petition bore 135,000 signatures and contained a long list of demands, including an end to the war with Japan and the granting of full political rights for all the czar's subjects.

The royal family had already moved to Tsarskoye Selo, their summer palace fifteen miles outside the city, when the demonstrators—ignorant of the imperial absence—began gathering soon after first light on Sunday, January 22. Dressed in their Sunday best and carrying religious banners and portraits of the czar, some 200,000 men, women, and children marched through the snowbound streets toward the Winter

Palace. At the sight of such a vast throng, the military authorities appear to have been seized by panic. They ordered the crowd to disperse, and when it refused to do so, volley after volley of rifle fire was poured into the marchers' ranks.

The casualties of Bloody Sunday, as it became known, totaled more than 1,000, including some 300 dead. Until now, most Russians had loyally supported the czar, blaming the shortcomings of the regime on Nicholas's advisers rather than on Nicholas himself. But the massacre outside the Winter Palace transformed the situation. "All classes condemn the authorities and more particularly the emperor," reported the United States Consul in Odessa. "The present ruler has lost absolutely the affection of the Russian people, and whatever the future may have in store for the dynasty, the present czar will never again be safe in the midst of his people."

The immediate consequence of Bloody Sunday was a veritable tornado of violence and disorder. In addition to strikes and demonstrations, there were mutinies in both the army and the navy; nationalist risings in Poland, the Baltic States, and the Caucasus; and an intensification of the SR terrorist campaign, which in February claimed as one of its victims Grand Duke Sergey, military commander of Moscow and the uncle of the czar. At the same time, under the influence of the SRs, the peasants rose up in discontent, burning manor houses, confiscating property, and refusing to work. The events of that autumn were more ominous still. On September 19, the printers of Moscow downed tools, setting off a chain reaction of sympathetic strikes. Factory workers and professionals alike gave support to the stoppage, bringing the country to a complete standstill.

There now appeared in a number of cities the first soviets—councils of workers' deputies elected to give a central direction to the strike. However, many of these bodies soon developed into alternative municipal governments, assuming powers

A peasant, his leave at an end, kneels to receive his father's blessing before returning to fight in the Great War. The war was initially welcomed by an outburst of patriotic fervor, but the mass conscriptions it occasioned soon became deeply unpopular. Some 15 million men were called up between 1914 and 1917, to fight in appalling conditions under poor leadership and incompetent administration. Their discontent manifested itself in a rash of riots, desertions, and self-inflicted injuries. Revolutionary agitators, conscripted wholesale by the government to remove the unhappy soldiers from the cities, found the demoralized military a perfect seedbed for their teachings.

that had hitherto been the exclusive preserve of imperial bureaucrats. The most effective was the Saint Petersburg soviet, made up of some 500 delegates representing about 250,000 workers. Based in the city's Technical Institute, it organized transport and supplies, recruited its own militia, arranged for guards and demonstrations, negotiated with employers and local council officials, and issued regular news and instructions through its own paper.

The local Mensheviks had taken the initiative in organizing the soviet, electing as president a former mathematics student named Leon Trotsky. Although with his pince-nez and cultivated manner he might have seemed more at home in a literary salon than on a barricade, Trotsky could claim a revolutionary record second to none. Even his name, originally Lev Bronstein, had been ironically changed to that of a former jailer. Since 1898—when he was first arrested, at the age of nineteen, for dissident activities—he had spent not a single year as a free man on Russian soil. When not in prison or Siberian exile, he had passed his time promoting the revolutionary cause from abroad. He had worked as a member of Lenin's *Iskra* group in London, but he had later sided with the Mensheviks, returning to support them upon the outbreak of revolutionary disturbances in 1905.

Initially the Bolsheviks were reluctant to join the Menshevik-dominated soviet; eventually, however, they agreed to do so, and the remainder of the strike saw the two Social Democrat factions working harmoniously with each other as well as with the Socialist Revolutionaries.

Outside Russia, nevertheless, relations between the left-wing factions were distinctly unfraternal—not least between the Bolsheviks and the Mensheviks. Although both groups welcomed what had become, in effect, a revolution against the czarist autocracy, they disagreed on the role the workers should play. To the Mensheviks, the revolution belonged essentially to the capitalist bourgeois class, and according to orthodox Marxist theory, this meant that the workers could play only a secondary role. Lenin had no intention, however, of playing a minor part in someone else's revolution (even if this meant revising Marxist doctrine), and he argued that the workers, in alliance with the peasants, would be strong enough to turn the revolution into a socialist one, thus bypassing the period of capitalism envisaged by Marx.

But Lenin made no quibble about the fact that, in order to take this historic shortcut, the workers would have to resort to armed force. He had spent some time in the Geneva public library studying textbooks on street fighting, and he bombarded his followers in Russia with instructions on how to conduct a guerrilla campaign. "It horrifies me—I give you my word—it horrifies me," he wrote to the Saint Petersburg Bolsheviks, "to find that there has been talk about bombs for *over six months,* yet not one has been made. . . . Form fighting squads *at once* everywhere." In a newspaper article, he urged the recruitment of a revolutionary army equipped with "rifles, revolvers, bombs, knives, knuckle-dusters, clubs, rags soaked in oil for starting fires, ropes or rope ladders, shovels for building barricades, dynamite cartridges, barbed wire, tacks against cavalry. . . ." He also suggested that funds for the uprising could be raised through "appropriation"—a euphemism for robbing banks.

Hopeful that the decisive phase of the struggle was about to begin, Lenin and Krupskaya returned in November to Saint Petersburg. But already the moment had passed. At the end of October, the czar had finally bowed to popular pressure by making what he called the "terrible decision" to grant a constitution. This provided for the setting up of an elected parliament, the Duma, and although it was to have only limited powers—Nicholas insisted that he was still supreme ruler—the prospect of even a modest step toward democracy was enough to turn back the revolutionary tide. The liberals withdrew their support of the general strike, workers began to drift back to the factories, the Saint Petersburg soviet was forcibly dissolved by troops, and Trotsky was arrested and subsequently exiled to Siberia. In the countryside, violence continued until 1907, but it was eventually brought under control by the massive use of military force.

Lenin spent the last weeks of 1905 attending a party conference in Finland, and it was from here that he and Krupskaya eventually made their way back to Geneva. "It is devilishly sad to have to return to this accursed Geneva again," he wrote to a colleague, "but there's no other way out!" Developments in Russia did little to dispel his gloom. Demoralized by the crushing of the Saint Petersburg and Moscow soviets, the workers showed no inclination to resume the struggle. As a result, there was a sharp decline in the number of those involved in strikes—from three million in 1905 to 46,000 in 1910. Despite a continuing campaign of political assassination, the active membership of the underground revolutionary groups also declined—from around 100,000 in 1905 to approximately 10,000 in 1910.

Even the peasants showed signs of becoming less militant, largely due to the actions of Nicholas's prime minister, Pyotr Stolypin. While ruthlessly suppressing peasant riots and executing hundreds by specially established court martials, he also instituted a major program of agrarian reform. Under Stolypin's policy, peasants were encouraged to break away from the commune and set up as independent farmers, with the right to buy and sell land. The intention was for the less able peasants to sell out and move into the towns, while the more able improved and expanded their holdings and thus acquired a strong stake in the existing order. As Stolypin put it, the government was relying "not on the feeble and drunk, but on the solid and strong."

Nevertheless, relative calm proved to be only temporary. In 1911, Stolypin was assassinated—on the order, rumor had it, of rivals in government—thus depriving the regime of its only effective leader. In addition, although they ameliorated the lot of the peasantry, Stolypin's reforms had done nothing for the urban proletariat, resulting in a resurgence of working-class militancy. Once again large-scale strikes became common, especially in Moscow and Saint Petersburg. Here, according to a government report, "the strike movement is definitely growing to threatening dimensions, more and more taking on a political coloring." The culmination came in July 1914, when the capital was paralyzed by a general walkout. Red flags fluttered over the barricades of overturned streetcars and telegraph poles, and workers and police fought hand-to-hand battles in the streets.

Not until August 1 and the outbreak of the Great War did the revolutionary fervor subside. The workers of Saint Petersburg and other Russian cities were now seized by a different kind of zeal, and the only demonstrations were those in favor of the czar and against the Germans and Austrians. The Bolsheviks, who openly criticized the war, were now the object of popular contempt, and those within reach of the Russian authorities were quickly rounded up and imprisoned. "During those wonderful early August days," wrote the British ambassador, Sir George Buchanan, "Russia seemed to have been completely transformed. . . . Instead of provoking a revolution, the war forged a new bond between sovereign and people."

But the bond was easily snapped. The world war was to prove the downfall of imperial Russia. It was not long before the Russian soldiers began to wonder if those

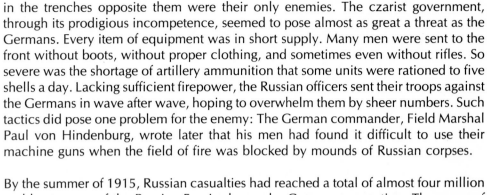

in the trenches opposite them were their only enemies. The czarist government, through its prodigious incompetence, seemed to pose almost as great a threat as the Germans. Every item of equipment was in short supply. Many men were sent to the front without boots, without proper clothing, and sometimes even without rifles. So severe was the shortage of artillery ammunition that some units were rationed to five shells a day. Lacking sufficient firepower, the Russian officers sent their troops against the Germans in wave after wave, hoping to overwhelm them by sheer numbers. Such tactics did pose one problem for the enemy: The German commander, Field Marshal Paul von Hindenburg, wrote later that his men had found it difficult to use their machine guns when the field of fire was blocked by mounds of Russian corpses.

By the summer of 1915, Russian casualties had reached a total of almost four million and huge areas of the Russian Empire lay under German occupation. The sense of panic and demoralization that now began to set in among the civilian population was exacerbated by the influx of millions of refugees from the fighting areas. The agriculture minister, A. V. Krivoshein, described how the refugees moved in a solid mass, treading down the fields and destroying the meadows and woods. "The railway lines are congested; even movements of military trains and shipments of food will soon become impossible. I do not know what is going on in the areas that fall into the hands of the enemy, but I do know that not only the immediate rear of our army but the remote rear as well are devastated, ruined."

In September, Nicholas assumed personal command of the armed forces and moved from the capital—which now had the less Germanic name of Petrograd—to his headquarters at Mogilev, on the Dnieper River. It was a calamitous decision. Not only was Nicholas totally inexperienced as a military commander, but in his absence, he left control of the country's domestic affairs to Czarina Alexandra—a figure only slightly less loathed in Russia than the kaiser himself. She was, indeed, a German princess by birth, and although she had shown almost fanatical devotion to her adopted homeland during her twenty-one years of marriage to the czar, there were many who doubted her loyalty in the present crisis.

But the main reason for the unpopularity of "the German woman" was her friendship with the self-proclaimed holy man Grigory Rasputin. A notorious drunkard and lecher, he had wormed his way into the empress's favor by using hypnotic powers to control the bleeding of her hemophiliac son, Alexis. She refused to make any important decision without first consulting her "beloved, never-to-be-forgotten teacher, savior, and mentor," and it was on Rasputin's advice that a succession of new ministers were now appointed. Some indication of their competence can be gleaned from the comments of a French dignitary who visited Petrograd in May 1916 and marveled that Russia "could permit itself the luxury of a government in which the premier was 'a disaster' and the minister of war 'a catastrophe.'"

The Russian aristocracy was particularly outraged at the power given to someone of Rasputin's lowly origins—he was the son of Siberian peasants—and appealed to the czar to intervene. But

The riveting gaze of Grigory Yefimovich Rasputin reveals the mesmeric powers that put the Russian royal family in his thrall. An uneducated Siberian peasant famed for his physical strength and erotic appetites, Rasputin arrived in Saint Petersburg in 1903 at the age of thirty-two, claiming to be a starets, or mendicant holy man. A prevailing cult of mysticism, combined with his ability to ease the hemophiliac czarevitch's bleeding, enabled Rasputin to gain the confidence of the royal family. Disgusted at his growing influence, a group of young nobles assassinated him on December 29, 1916. A man of enormous energy, he proved difficult to kill: He was poisoned with cyanide, shot three times at close range, then bound and thrown, still alive, into the Neva River. He drowned, but according to one account, he managed to untie the knots before he died.

Nicholas preferred to be guided by the czarina, and she had no intention of abandoning her prophet. "Don't yield," she exhorted Nicholas. "Be the master. Obey your firm little wife and our friend. Believe in us."

In December 1916, a group of young nobles took matters into their own hands and murdered Rasputin. Although their action won widespread approval, it did nothing to restore public confidence in the czar. The war continued to go badly, and the mood of despair engendered by military defeat was compounded by increasing unrest in the cities. Food was scarce, and large numbers of peasants—mostly women—poured into the towns looking for employment, where they were forced to live and work in conditions of dreadful squalor.

On March 8, 1917, the storm of revolution broke. It started with a group of female protestors demonstrating against poor living conditions, and soon thousands of striking workers were marching through the streets of Petrograd calling for bread and peace and singing the "Marseillaise," the anthem of the French Revolution. The following day, the crowds began attacking municipal buildings and police stations,

Demonstrators scatter in the streets of Petrograd during the 1917 pro-Bolshevik uprising known as the July Days. Between July 16 and 17, about 150 people were killed or injured in street fighting as mobs of disaffected soldiers and factory workers demonstrated against the provisional government. The rioting was short-lived, and the ensuing backlash against the Bolsheviks forced Lenin to flee the country. The July Days, however, demonstrated the vulnerability of the provisional government, setting the stage for a revolution three months later in which the Bolsheviks finally seized power.

and by March 10, large areas of the city were in the hands of the workers.

At nine o'clock that evening, the czar, who was at army headquarters in Mogilev, telegraphed the commander of the Petrograd garrison to suppress the rioters by force. But many of the troops called out to restore order refused to fire on the strikers—many, indeed, took their side. And by the end of the next day, the majority of the 170,000-strong garrison had joined the mutiny.

Unable to control the chaos, the czar's ministers either fled the city or went underground, leaving a power vacuum into which the party leaders of the Duma felt obliged to step. At around midnight on March 12, they formed an emergency committee to restore order in the capital, and three days later, this was turned into a provisional government under the premiership of a prominent liberal, Prince Georgy Lvov. Within hours, the new government had dispatched two Duma deputies to Pskov, where striking railway workers had forced the czar's train to halt on its return journey from Mogilev. Until now, Nicholas had treated the Duma with open contempt, often ignoring its decisions, and twice dissolving it altogether. He received the two deputies with courtesy, however, and readily agreed to their request that he should abdicate. (He had already been told by his generals that they could no longer give him their support.)

His only objection was to the proposal that his son, Alexis, should succeed him. The boy was still in delicate health, and Nicholas felt that the burden of monarchy would be too great for him. It was agreed, therefore, that the crown should pass to Nicholas's brother, Grand Duke Michael. But on the next day, March 16, the grand duke refused the offer, and the 1,000-year-old Russian monarchy came to an end.

The new government seemed to have established itself with remarkable ease. The upper echelons of the army pledged their support, the officials of the old regime agreed to carry on with their duties, and the apparatus of the state continued to function very much as before. The apparent calm was, however, deceptive. The real arbiter of the nation's fate would prove to be not the provisional government but the Petrograd Soviet of Workers' and Soldiers' Deputies. As the new war minister, Alexander Guchkov, explained to the army chief of staff:

The provisional government does not possess any real power; and its directives are carried out only to the extent that it is permitted by the soviet . . . which enjoys all the essential elements of real power, since the troops, the railways, the post, and telegraph are all in its hands. One can say flatly that the provisional government exists only so long as it is permitted by the soviet.

As in 1905, the leaders of the soviet were mainly Mensheviks and SRs, and although they distrusted the liberal-dominated government, they were content for it to carry through the "bourgeois" democratic reforms that would, they believed, pave the way for a future socialist revolution. In this they were supported by the Petrograd Bolsheviks, whose leaders, Lev Kamenev and Joseph Stalin, pledged support for the provisional government. From Lenin, seething with impatience

Moscow street urchins, heads shaved to prevent lice, stand by the crown of a toppled statue of Czar Alexander III, father of Nicholas II. An April 1918 decree authorized the destruction of all czarist memorials and their replacement with statues of revolutionary heroes.

in Switzerland, this approach drew nothing but scorn. His belief now, as during the crisis of twelve years before, was that the workers in Russia, led, of course, by the Bolsheviks, should seize control of the state immediately. In a message to the Petrograd comrades, he summed up Bolshevik tactics as "no rapprochement with other parties" and "no trust and no support for the new government."

The government immediately found itself in trouble. In April, when Foreign Minister Miliukov released a note promising solidarity with the Allied powers, the war-weary population rose in mass demonstrations. The government was forced to reshuffle and entered a coalition with the soviet to strengthen its base.

Lenin was desperate to be in Petrograd, but the problem of finding a safe route through war-torn Europe seemed insoluble. It was the Germans who provided the answer, offering to transport Lenin by rail across Germany to the Baltic coast. Throughout the war, Berlin had been channeling money to several Russian revolutionary groups, including the Bolsheviks, and it saw Lenin's return to Russia as an excellent way of making trouble for the provisional government. The only proviso was that Lenin remain incommunicado during his passage through Germany.

Setting out from Zurich on April 9, Lenin and a group of companions—traveling in a locked and guarded carriage on a train specially provided for them by the German authorities—reached Stockholm five days later. In the words of the British statesman Winston Churchill, they had been transported through German territory "in a sealed truck like a plague bacillus." Here they stopped long enough for Lenin to buy a new pair of shoes, on the advice of a companion who said that a man in public life ought to look the part. (Lenin turned down the suggestion that he also buy an overcoat and extra underwear, declaring that he was "not going to Petrograd to open a tailor's shop.")

From Stockholm, the party was taken by train to the Finnish frontier, where they boarded another train for Petrograd. As they drew closer to the capital, there was increasing speculation about the kind of reception that awaited them. Lenin thought it quite possible that they would all be arrested for high treason for accepting help from an enemy power. Their fears were quickly dispelled, however, when the train steamed into Petrograd's Finland station on April 16.

The station and its approaches were thronged with supporters who greeted Lenin like a returning hero. He was carried shoulder-high from the platform to the station hall, where a band struck up a thunderous rendition of the "Marseillaise." Shepherded into the former imperial waiting room, he received a chary welcome from Nikolay Chkheidze, Menshevik chairman of the Petrograd soviet, who made a conciliatory speech, urging that the two parties close ranks. But Lenin pointedly ignored Chkheidze and instead spoke to the milling crowd outside, denouncing the "piratical imperialist war" and warning against the "sweet promises" of the provisional government.

Later that night, Lenin addressed an impromptu meeting of party members at the sumptuous Kshesinskaya Mansion, erstwhile home of the czar's favorite ballerina but now requisitioned to serve as the Bolsheviks' headquarters. The only way to end the war, Lenin asserted, was for the soviets of workers', soldiers', and peasants' deputies throughout the country to overthrow the provisional government and take control

His face cast half in shadow, Lenin stares enigmatically at the viewer in a studio portrait taken in July 1920. Born on April 22, 1870, he was the grandson of a doctor, and the son of a school inspector and a teacher. Lenin became a committed revolutionary following the execution of his brother for terrorist activities in 1887. Four years later, he graduated from Saint Petersburg University with a law degree, and it was while he was working as a public defender that he first made contact with groups of revolutionary Marxists. After his rise to power in October 1917, he successfully guided Russia through civil war and economic collapse until his death on January 21, 1924. His image was to become a worldwide icon of revolution.

themselves. Instead of a parliamentary republic, he advocated a soviet republic, which would nationalize the land and the banks, take over the production and distribution of goods, and replace the existing police force, army, and bureaucracy with proletarian institutions. Meanwhile, it was the task of the Bolsheviks to criticize and expose the shortcomings of their opponents—including the "social lackeys" who made up the present leadership of the Petrograd soviet.

Among those listening to Lenin's two-hour tirade was a Menshevik, Nikolay Sukhanov, who had slipped into the meeting past the Bolshevik guards. "I shall never forget that thunderlike speech . . .," he wrote. "It seemed as though all the elements had risen from their abodes, and the spirit of universal destruction, knowing neither barriers nor doubts, neither human difficulties nor human calculations, was hovering around Kshesinskaya's reception room above the heads of the bewitched delegates."

Beyond Kshesinskaya's reception room, the spell was less potent. In demanding a second revolution, Lenin seemed, in the view of many Bolsheviks, to have lost touch with political reality. At a meeting of the Petrograd central committee on the following afternoon, his program was unceremoniously rejected. (One critic described it as "the delirium of a madman.") Lenin persisted, however, and by the month of May, most of his program had been accepted as party policy. It was now that the party's fortunes began to rise. A disastrous offensive against the Germans in June led to further discontent and desertions among the military forces, and as the provisional government failed to introduce radical reforms, increasing numbers of workers, soldiers, and peasants rallied to the Bolshevik slogans of Peace, Land, and Bread and All Power to the Soviets.

The rising popularity of the Bolsheviks was manifested on July 16, when for two days, armed mobs roamed the streets of Petrograd, demanding that the soviet take power. The rioting died down of its own accord, but the provisional government, which blamed the Bolsheviks for the uprising, reacted sharply. The party's headquarters were raided, its newspaper, *Pravda*, was closed down, and several of its leaders were arrested. More serious, the government also published a number of documents—some forged, some genuine—purporting to show that Lenin was a German spy. So loud was the outcry against him that the Bolshevik central committee feared for his life. He went into immediate hiding, and at the beginning of August, dressed in the clothes of a worker and with his distinctive beard shaved off, he crossed the border into Finland.

Silencing the Bolsheviks, however, could not prevent Russia's continued plunge into chaos. There was a resurgence of strikes and lockouts, and peasants, unwilling to wait any longer for the government to introduce agrarian reform, began seizing and plundering the landlords' estates. Another threat to law and order was the increasing number of army deserters drifting back from the front. By August, it was estimated that two million of them were roaming the streets, terrorizing the population with attacks on person and property alike.

An additional menace came at the end of August, when the right-wing General Lavr Kornilov attempted to mount a coup. Threatening to hang every member of the soviet, he ordered his troops to march on Petrograd. They did not get far. The divided socialists now rallied behind the government. Railway workers refused to move Kornilov's units, telegraphers would not send his messages, and eventually his own troops defected. With the fear of counterrevolution came a fresh upsurge of support for the Bolsheviks, who in September won control of both the Petrograd and Moscow

A pince-nez adds a touch of elegance to Leon Trotsky's plain revolutionary garb in this studiedly casual portrait. Born on November 7, 1879, he was the son of a Ukrainian farmer. Trotsky plunged into revolutionary activities at the age of nineteen. His brilliance as an orator and administrator ensured his rapid rise through the socialist ranks. A vehement supporter of Lenin and one of the most important figures in the Bolshevik government, Trotsky used his organizational abilities to set up the Red Army and steer it to victory in the civil war that followed the revolution. He was later outmaneuvered by his rival, Joseph Stalin, in the struggle for leadership of the Communist party after Lenin's death. Exiled in 1929, Trotsky was assassinated in 1940.

soviets. From Lenin, still hiding out in Finland, this drew a barrage of revolutionary exhortations. Writing to the Bolshevik central committee in Petrograd, he urged it to make immediate preparations for an armed uprising. "History will not forgive us," he declared, "if we do not seize power now."

The central committee was more cautious, however, and it was not until October 23 that the momentous decision was made. Lenin, still clean shaven and wearing a wig, returned from his Finnish haven to take part in the debate. This proved to be a passionate and sometimes angry affair, but after ten hours, the committee agreed by ten votes to two "that an armed uprising is inevitable and the time is perfectly ripe." At 3:00 a.m. the meeting broke up, and Lenin made his way back to a secret address in Vyborg, a working-class suburb of Petrograd.

The details of the uprising were left to a Military Revolutionary Committee (MRC). Prominent among its members was Leon Trotsky. Having escaped from Siberia in 1907, Trotsky had spent ten years as a revolutionary émigré in Europe and the United States, before returning to Russia in March 1917, where he had assumed control of a left-wing Menshevik group that sided with the Bolsheviks.

The date for the uprising was tentatively set for November 6, the day before the second All-Russian Congress of Soviets was due to meet in Petrograd. Although most of the delegates were likely to be Bolsheviks, it was Lenin's intention that the Congress, "irrespective of its composition, would be confronted with a situation in which

Revolutionary workers, executed by Austrian troops in 1918, hang from a line of gibbets in Yekaterinoslav in the southern Ukraine. During the civil war that broke out in 1917, Russia's Bolshevik government had to fight not only czarist forces but also foreign powers intent on restoring the old order. In the east, Czech and Japanese troops occupied Siberia; from the Arctic ports of Archangel and Murmansk, British, American, and French forces threatened northern Russia; and German and Austrian units marched in from the west. By the summer of 1918, no fewer than eighteen insurgent governments were competing with that of Moscow. It was not until 1920 that the Bolsheviks finally regained control of the country, consolidating it three years later as the Union of Soviet Socialist Republics.

the seizure of power by the workers is an actual fact.'' In the event, it was the provisional government—now under the leadership of its war minister, Alexander Kerensky, who had replaced Prince Lvov following the July riots—that delivered the first blow. Early in the morning of November 6, the government declared a state of insurrection. The MRC was outlawed, and warrants were issued for the arrest of Trotsky and other Bolshevik leaders.

To Lenin, isolated in Vyborg, it was clear only that the government had taken action. He had no idea how the party or the MRC was responding, and he feared that the Bolsheviks might miss their opportunity. The government had cut the telephone links with the Smolny Institute, a former girls' school that was now the headquarters of both the party and the Petrograd soviet, so a messenger was dispatched from Vyborg to carry Lenin's last-minute appeal to the central committee: ''With all my power I wish to persuade the comrades that now everything hangs on a hair. . . . We must at all costs, this evening, tonight, arrest the ministers. . . . We must not wait!! We may lose everything.''

The appeal was scarcely on its way when Lenin, unable to contain his anxiety, set off for Smolny. Traveling part of the way on foot, part by streetcar, he arrived there just before midnight. At first, the sentries refused him admission—he was wearing a wig and the lower part of his face was disguised by a bandage—but finally they allowed him to pass. He immediately headed for the room where Trotsky was working. By now it was November 7—October 25, according to the old Russian calendar—which happened to be Trotsky's thirty-eighth birthday. In answer to Lenin's questions, he explained that, within the next two hours, detachments of revolutionary troops and armed workers would start occupying the railway stations, power plants, post offices, telephone exchanges, and other key points of the city. At 2:00 a.m. Trotsky pulled out his watch and said, ''It's begun.'' Lenin replied, ''From being on the run to supreme power—that's too much. It makes me dizzy.'' Then, according to Trotsky, he made the sign of the cross.

The provisional government, unable to rely on the regular troops of the Petrograd garrison, had entrusted the city's security to 2,000 officer-cadets drafted in from Oranienbaum. They showed little inclination to fight, however, and by 10:00 a.m., the MRC forces had taken all but one of their objectives. The exception was the Winter Palace, where the remaining members of the government were holding out, guarded by cadets and Amazons—a volunteer force of patriotic women who had sworn to fight to the death against the Germans and other enemies of the state. At about 11:00 p.m., the guns in the nearby Saint Peter and Saint Paul Fortress began a desultory shelling of the palace, and three hours later, its defenders gave up without a struggle. Bursting into the small room where the government ministers were gathered, an MRC member, Vladimir Antonov-Ovseyenko, shouted, ''In the name of the Military Revolutionary Committee of the Petrograd soviet, I declare the provisional government deposed. You are all under arrest.'' (One of those absent from this early-morning drama was Prime Minister Kerensky, who had fled the city the previous morning in a car provided by the American ambassador.)

The soviet victory was now complete. It had taken just forty-eight hours and cost fewer than twenty casualties. As Trotsky himself later put it: ''The final act of the revolution seems, after all this, too brief, too dry, too businesslike—somehow out of correspondence with the historic scope of the events.''

At 8:40 that night, Lenin, now chairman of the Council of People's Commissars—the Bolshevik cabinet—rose to address the All-Russian Congress of Soviets. Crammed into the former ballroom of the Smolny Institute, and almost suffocating in the clouds of tobacco smoke that swirled beneath the glazed white chandeliers, the delegates had opened their first session just as the bombardment of the Winter Palace was getting under way. Almost immediately, a large body of Mensheviks and Socialist Revolutionaries had walked out in protest at the Bolsheviks' actions. Most delegates had chosen to remain, however, and they now greeted Lenin with rapturous applause. He stood there, wrote the American left-wing journalist John Reed, "gripping the edge of the reading stand, letting his little winking eyes travel over the crowd . . . apparently oblivious to the long-rolling ovation, which lasted several minutes. When it finished he said simply, 'We shall now proceed to construct the socialist order!' Again that overwhelming roar."

Over the next few weeks, the Council of People's Commissars was in session for six hours a day, issuing a series of decrees intended to sweep away the accumulated customs and institutions of centuries. The land, the banks, the merchant marine, and all industrial enterprises were taken into state ownership; all military ranks and insignia were abolished and all military formations subordinated to elected committees of soldiers or sailors; the existing judicial institutions were replaced by "people's courts" and "revolutionary tribunals," whose members were elected by the local population; the Church was permitted to continue, but its vast holdings were confiscated and religious teaching was forbidden in schools. On a more personal level, men and women were declared equal in law, receiving equal pay, and the strict czarist code governing marriage and divorce was abolished. Working women were to be entitled to sixteen weeks' paid maternity leave, eight weeks before and eight weeks after the birth of the baby.

With this newfound freedom came a more relaxed attitude toward sexual morals. Free love was very popular among younger socialists, but the older party members, including Lenin, frowned on this behavior—just as they deplored the nudists who, in order to express their ideologic commitment, sometimes jumped naked onto the streetcars of Moscow.

The new regime was generally welcomed in the towns but attracted only lukewarm support in the countryside, where the traditional champions of the peasants, the Socialist Revolutionaries, were still in the ascendant. They were never, however, to transform their popularity into power. At the first meeting of the Constituent Assembly of all socialist parties, held on January 18, 1918, at the Tauride Palace in Petrograd, the building was surrounded by armed Bolshevik troops. Additional troops occupied the galleries of the debating chamber, and when a motion endorsing the authority of the new Bolshevik-led government was rejected, the meeting was forcibly adjourned. The doors were then sealed, and a group of SR demonstrators who had turned up outside the palace was dispersed with gunfire. To Lenin, the end of the assembly meant "a complete and frank liquidation of the ideas of formal democracy in the name of revolutionary dictatorship. It will serve as a good lesson."

A much more serious danger to the regime was the German army, which, unconcerned by the niceties of revolutionary dogma, had occupied large tracts of Russian territory in Poland and the Baltic regions. At the All-Russian Congress in November, Lenin had called for "a just and democratic peace," without annexations or indemnities. He had hoped to spark revolutions in the other belligerent countries, which

would lead to the setting up of socialist governments throughout Europe. His peace appeal had been ignored, however, so in December, a Russian delegation led by Trotsky, the newly appointed commissar for foreign affairs, had begun negotiations for a separate peace with Germany.

By now, the Russian army had all but disintegrated, and the Germans were demanding a heavy price for ending hostilities. Plunged into a turmoil of indecision, the Bolshevik leadership was still debating the issue when, on February 18, the Germans resumed their offensive. Five days later, with their troops driving deep into the Ukraine, they presented a new and even tougher set of demands. Some members of the central committee proposed waging a guerrilla war, but Lenin insisted that capitulation was the only sure way to safeguard the revolution. He finally forced through a decision for acceptance by threatening to resign.

The peace treaty with the Central Powers—Germany, Austria, and Turkey—was signed at the Polish town of Brest Litovsk (now the Russian town of Brest) on March 3. By its terms, Russia had to yield large amounts of territory in the Baltic, Finland, Poland, Ukraine, and the Caucasus. The losses cost Russia one-third of its agricultural land and its population; more than four-fifths of its coal mines; almost one-quarter of its railways; and one-third of its factories. Russia was also required to make reparations payments of six billion marks.

Far from bringing a respite in Russia's suffering, the Treaty of Brest Litovsk was to signal the start of a bloody civil war. Within three months of signing the agreement, the Soviet government was again fighting for survival—this time against anti-Bolshevik Russians known as the Whites. Led by former officers of the czar, and conspicuously supplied by the Western Allies, who hoped to bring Russia back into the war against Germany, the White armies launched offensives from the east, the northwest, and the south. For a while it seemed as if the new socialist state would fall. In the summer of 1918, White forces occupied much of east Russia and came within 300 miles of Moscow—to which the capital had been transferred on March 11.

To combat this threat, the Bolsheviks quickly built up their own ''Red'' army, under

While held in the Siberian town of Tobolsk, the czar and his children assemble for a photograph on a platform set above their greenhouse roof. Moved to Tobolsk in August 1917 from their summer palace of Tsarskoye Selo, the royal family's life in captivity was relatively tranquil: The children took lessons with their tutor; the czarina read, embroidered, or painted; and Nicholas walked in the compound or sawed logs—the platform above the greenhouse was his handiwork. In April 1918, however, the imperial family was relocated to the Urals town of Ekaterinburg, where they were murdered by members of the local soviet on July 16.

Female workers and peasants are exhorted to "form ranks with men under the red banner and terrify the bourgeoisie."

РАБОТНИЦЫ И КРЕСТЬЯНКИ
ВСЕ НА ВЫБОРЫ

Под КРАСНЫЙ СТЯГ, В РЯДЫ С МУЖЧИНОЙ! – БУРЖУАЗИИ СТРАХ НЕСЕМ!

Российская Социалистическая Федеративная Советская Республика

КОММУНИСТ УКАЗЫВАЕТ ВРАГА И ВЕДЕТ В БОЙ

РАБОЧЕ-КРЕСТЬЯНСКАЯ ОБОРОНА

СОВЕТСКАЯ РОС
осажденный ЛАГЕ
ВСЕ НА

The Red Army s
is adapted to remi
everyone that "Russ
is an armed camp.

THE ART OF AGIT-PROP

In the war years following 1917, agitational propaganda, or "agit-prop," played a vital part in spreading the revolutionary message. Speeches and rallies were combined with colorful posters and easily remembered slogans to bring Bolshevik theories to the largely illiterate masses.

Rosta, the Moscow-based Russian Telegraph Agency, became an important propaganda arm. Telegraphs informed artists in every major city of news, topics, and slogans that were then turned into brilliantly colored posters called Rosta windows.

In the countryside, special "agit-trains" distributed Bolshevik literature. Painted with revolutionary images, such trains carried mobile presses capable of producing newspaper runs of 15,000 copies. All had bookshops, and some contained movie theaters with seats for up to 150 people. In 1920, there was even an "agit-ship" that toured the Volga and Kama rivers.

ПЕТРОГРАДА НЕ ОТДАДИМ

Soldiers, sailors, and workers unite under the words, "We will not surrender Petrograd."

Standard-bearing Russians carry the message of international communism.

LONG LIVE THE THIRD COMMUNIST INTERNATIONAL!
EVVIVA IL TERZA INTERNAZIONALE COMMUNISTA!
VIVE LA TROISIEME INTERNATIONALE COMMUNISTE!
ES LEBE DIE DRITTE KOMMUNISTISCHE INTERNATIONALE!

A sword-wielding worker commemorates the second anniversary of the October Revolution.

Вторая годовщина великой октябрьской революции.

A Rosta window exhorts people to "work with your rifle beside you."

РАБОТАТЬ НАДО
ВИНТОВКА-РЯДОМ
ПЕТЕРБУРГ РОСТА.

the direction of Trotsky, now commissar for war. Although Trotsky recruited as many party members as possible, he soon found that they lacked the necessary military experience for leadership. Accordingly he conscripted large numbers of former imperial army officers, whose anti-Bolshevik sentiments were forgotten in the face of Trotsky's open threats to the safety of their wives and children. To discourage desertion and spying, he also appointed military commissars—political agents whose job was to supervise the army commanders. Steaming from crisis point to crisis point in a special armored train—pulled by two engines and equipped with a radio, generating plant, printing press, garage, and squad of machine gunners—Trotsky exhorted his men with fiery rhetoric and threats. Strict discipline was maintained; if a unit deserted, Trotsky was perfectly capable of having the commanding officer, commissars, and one in ten of the soldiers shot.

With the civil war came a rising tide of political violence. Socialist Revolutionaries, bent on sabotaging the Treaty of Brest Litovsk, assassinated the German ambassador, as well as several leading Communists. In August 1918, one female assailant even succeeded in wounding Lenin himself. The Communists replied with an avowed campaign of Red Terror, aimed at wiping out all opposition—real or imagined. Thousands were rounded up and summarily executed by the regime's new security police, the Cheka. The Whites applied the same ruthless tactics, shooting prisoners and hostages and killing suspected Communists without trial.

Among the earliest victims of this savagery were the czar and his family. Following Nicholas's abdication, the seven Romanovs had been shunted from Tsarskoye Selo to the small Siberian town of Tobolsk, and from there to the mining center of Ekaterinburg in the Urals, where they were installed in a wealthy merchant's house—the House of Special Purpose, as it was ominously dubbed by the hostile local soviet. With the coming to power of the Bolsheviks, the family's conditions had rapidly deteriorated: They were now forced to take their meals out of a common pot, and all but their doctor and two servants were sent away. The end came on July 16, 1918. On that day, the family members were told that they were to be moved again, and they did not go to bed. Late in the evening, they were ordered down to the cellar, along with their doctor and the two servants. Here, three chairs were put out—one each for Nicholas, his wife, and their sick son, fourteen-year-old Alexis, who had to be carried downstairs by his father. The head guard, Yurovsky, read out a sentence of execution that, he said, had been passed by the Ekaterinburg soviet.

He then shot Nicholas dead, and his companions fired a volley at the rest of the family. Alexis did not die at once, and Yurovsky emptied his pistol into the boy. Anastasia, the youngest daughter, also remained alive, and was dispatched with a bayonet. Even the children's spaniel was killed, its skull smashed by a rifle butt. The bodies were taken by truck to a nearby mine shaft, where for three days they were burned with gasoline and sulfuric acid. Whatever still remained of the corpses was then lowered into the mine.

Occupied with the horrors of civil war, the Russian people had little sympathy to spare for the victims of Ekaterinburg. In November 1918, with the surrender of Germany, the Allied powers decided on a policy of armed intervention against the Soviet government. Troops from fourteen countries were sent to assist the Whites. But the Red Army fought back with grim tenacity, and by the end of 1920, it had achieved complete victory.

Despite the ravages of war, the last three years had endorsed Lenin's version of traditional Marxist doctrine, whereby the proletariat and peasantry together had been able to complete the revolution. The country over which the Bolsheviks now presided, however, was in a state of virtual collapse. The towns were hungry and half-empty, the railways were breaking down, and industry was almost at a standstill, with industrial production less than one-third of its 1913 level. The shortage of goods, plus the government's propensity to print more and more money, caused chronic inflation. As money lost its significance, barter became the basic form of exchange, and the roads of Russia became jammed with *mesochniki,* or bagmen, trundling objects from the city to the countryside to swap for food. One story tells of a bewildered peasant who was offered a grand piano in exchange for a sack of grain. Even the government relied on barter, paying wages partly in food, goods, and services such as the use of streetcars.

While this so-called War Communism was welcomed by some Bolsheviks, who felt that money had no place in socialist society, for most of the population it produced terrible hardship, which was not alleviated by two consecutive years of drought and famine. Deaths from hunger and disease in 1921 and 1922 were to total some five million—more than the combined military casualties for the Great War and the civil war. The mood of discontent was fueled by the regime's increasing use of coercion. The peasants were particularly incensed at the compulsory requisitioning of their grain supplies, and there were armed uprisings in the Ukraine, the northern Caucasus, and western Siberia. In March 1921, there was even a rebellion by the sailors of the Kronstadt naval base. The Kronstadters had long been among the Bolsheviks' firmest supporters, but now they were denouncing "the arbitrary rule of the commissars" and calling for a true soviet republic of workers and peasants.

The government, unrestrained by sentiment, dispatched 25,000 Red Army troops to put down the Kronstadt mutineers. However, it was clear to Lenin that, in order to prevent further chaos and bloodshed, the regime would have to adopt a more moderate economic approach. This was embodied in a series of measures that were to become known as the New Economic Policy, or NEP. Grain requisitioning was replaced by a tax in kind, with the peasants allowed to sell for profit whatever was surplus to their own requirements. Most trading and small-scale industrial enterprises were returned to private hands, and the state-owned sector was encouraged to restore profit-and-loss accounting to its operations.

The rapid increase in agricultural and industrial production that ensued was accompanied by other benefits. The government spent increasing sums on health, housing, and education. Indeed, progressive methods in schools and the treatment of orphans—there were thousands left over from the world war and the civil war—and delinquents excited interest in the West. On the negative side, food rationing, austerity, and unemployment meant that the hardships were far from over. State defense contracts had ended with the cease-fire of 1917, and the excess manpower that this caused ensured that wages remained low. As late as 1925, the pay of miners, metal workers, and engine drivers was less than it had been before 1914.

Worse still was the lot of the Orthodox clergy. Distrusted on both religious and political grounds, they were reduced to the state of *lishentsy,* or "deprivees," robbed of their voting rights, and subjected to higher taxes and lower rations than other members of the community. Their children were barred from specialist or higher education. Moreover, the discrimination was often accompanied by violence from zealous Communists, operating with the tacit approval of the authorities. Many church buildings were desecrated or destroyed, and a large number of priests were beaten up or killed. By 1921, twenty-eight bishops and more than 1,000 priests had been arrested or had died as a result of violence.

This attitude of intolerance reached to the very heights of government. In March 1921, at the Tenth Party Congress, Lenin announced a ban on all official opposition groups within the party, and he reduced its membership by almost 50 percent. The remaining members of the Communist party (as the Bolsheviks were now called) were rendered powerless, bound by the decisions of the central committee—in effect, Lenin himself. It was the final vindication of the elitist policies Lenin had espoused at the Second Congress twenty years earlier. Under the autocracy of the czars, the Russian people had been told what to do; now, under the virtual dictatorship of Lenin, they were increasingly being told what to think. Russia was on the road to becoming a totalitarian state.

It was not Lenin, however, who would lead the country down that road. Over the

Wrapped against the January cold, mourners line up outside Moscow's Great Hall of the Trade Unions in 1924 to view Lenin's embalmed body lying in state. Unlike the simple cremations accorded to other revolutionary leaders, Lenin's mourning rites were organized on the lavish scale considered fitting for a man intended to become a revolutionary legend. The stage manager of this process of image building was Joseph Stalin, who was later, in 1929, to erect an imposing, red granite mausoleum in Moscow's Red Square where Lenin's body could be permanently displayed. Ironically, Lenin himself had come to distrust Stalin; the year before Lenin died, he had sought to find ways of removing Stalin from his Communist-party post.

next three years, the seemingly innocuous figure of Joseph Stalin would emerge as the arbiter of Russia's future. Although Lenin was only fifty-one, at the time of the Tenth Congress, the cares and burdens of the past few years had taken their toll. The following May, he suffered a stroke, the first of a series that would paralyze him and steadily reduce his ability to make decisions.

Despite his disability, Lenin was still officially head of the government. But other prominent party members were now jockeying for power. The two main contenders who emerged in the struggle for succession were the charismatic Trotsky and the apparently dull and pedestrian Stalin. Unlike Trotsky, Stalin was a bureaucrat rather than a thinker or a man of action—his nickname was Comrade Card-Index. But he was a master of intrigue, a quality that, combined with immense patience, had gained him the post of general secretary of the Communist party.

Stalin's influence won the day, and the central committee duly elected him as a member of a temporary triumvirate that would steer Russia through Lenin's illness. Under the guidance of the triumvirate, the process of centralization that Lenin had initiated accelerated rapidly; bureaucracy flourished, as Stalin spread the tentacles of his influence through the party machine; and early in 1923, regional minorities, who had gained a measure of independence during the civil war, were heavy-handedly forced to join Russia in the Union of Soviet Socialist Republics.

By that time, Lenin was sinking fast, his strokes having denied him of even the ability to write. Nevertheless, in the winter of 1922-1923, he mustered the strength to dictate a number of articles in which he voiced his fears for the stability of the party. He saw that the state had become a mass of red tape and incompetence; furthermore, the increased centralization had robbed regional and representative bodies of their power. He reserved his strongest criticism for Stalin, claiming that he was too crude to lead the revolution into the future, and urging the party to remove him from office. On March 10, however, another stroke deprived him of the power of speech, and his political life came to an end. He died on January 21 the following year.

In the aftermath of Lenin's death, Stalin began systematically removing all potential rivals. With his supporters positioned in every part of the party, Stalin easily dominated the other two members of the triumvirate. And by December 1927, Stalin had such a large following that he was able to engineer the mass expulsion of all opposition groups from the Communist party. Two years later, his last opponent, Trotsky, was outmaneuvered, discredited, and banished. He was assassinated in Mexico, on Stalin's orders, eleven years later.

Now Stalin was the absolute ruler, and he set about remodeling the Soviet Union according to his own vision. The New Economic Policy was abandoned, to be replaced by a system of state-organized industry and collective agriculture. It was, in effect, a revolution even more devastating than that of 1917. Stalin's policies would succeed in making the Soviet Union a modern, industrialized nation, but the cost in human suffering would surpass the harshest excesses of the czars. For a quarter of a century, the Russian people would endure the tyranny of one of the most formidable dictators the world had ever known.

THE MIDDLE EAST TRANSFORMED

3 The most beautiful women in the world come from the Circassian villages north of the Caucasus Mountains. Or so, at least, had thought generations of Ottoman sultans, who for centuries had seized or purchased the fair-skinned Circassians to be installed in their harems. Indeed, at the turn of the twentieth century, the eunuchs of Sultan Abdul Hamid II guarded an establishment of some 200 such odalisques. Accordingly, the Circassian villagers were surprised to receive, in the summer of 1909, a message from the Ottoman government asking them to come and take their women back. And the Circassians were not alone: Throughout the Ottoman Empire, newspapers carried advertisements inviting anyone whose daughters or sisters were in the harem to come to Constantinople at the government's expense and claim his relatives.

It was not that Abdul Hamid wanted a change of harem, as had many of his ancestors; nor was it that he could no longer afford to maintain such a large establishment. It was not even that the sixty-six-year-old ruler had become tired of sex. It was simply that on April 29, the sultan had been deposed. That in itself was nothing new. Of the thirty-three Ottoman sultans who had ruled since the first of the line, Osman I, came to power in 1300, ten had been deposed. But power had always remained in the hands of a sultan. Now, however, as a group of shabbily dressed Circassians waited expectantly in Constantinople's Topkapi Palace to collect their relatives, the presiding official did not represent the administration of the incoming sultan. He was instead a parliamentary commissioner, a member of the Committee of Union and Progress, or, as the inhabitants of Constantinople would have known him, a Young Turk.

With Abdul Hamid's deposal, the Ottoman sultanate had effectively ended. Other sultans would follow, but they would be mere figureheads. Beginning in 1909, it was to be the Young Turks who would rule the Ottoman Empire, replacing six centuries of despotism with representative government. Their rule, however, was to be short-lived. By 1918, drawn into the maelstrom of the Great War, the Ottoman Empire lay in pieces. From the rubble emerged a patchwork of fiercely nationalistic states, whose conflicting interests were to shape the future of the Middle East. And of these, none was more vociferously independent than the Republic of Turkey. Over the next decade, this last rump of the Ottoman Empire was to undergo a thorough program of Westernization and industrialization, which would see the final abolition of the sultanate and the rise to power of Mustafa Kemal, who became known as Kemal Atatürk, the father of modern Turkey.

At its height, during the sixteenth and early seventeenth centuries, the Ottoman Empire had seemed invincible. Its territories encircled the eastern Mediterranean in an unbroken chain from Algeria to Greece and the Balkan states that bordered

The figure of Mustafa Kemal, a cigarette holder poised in his hand, dominates a group of fellow Ottoman officers photographed in 1915 on the Gallipoli Peninsula, in the course of the Great War campaign that brought him victory and fame. An implacable Turkish nationalist, Kemal founded the Republic of Turkey in 1923, following the postwar collapse of the Ottoman Empire.

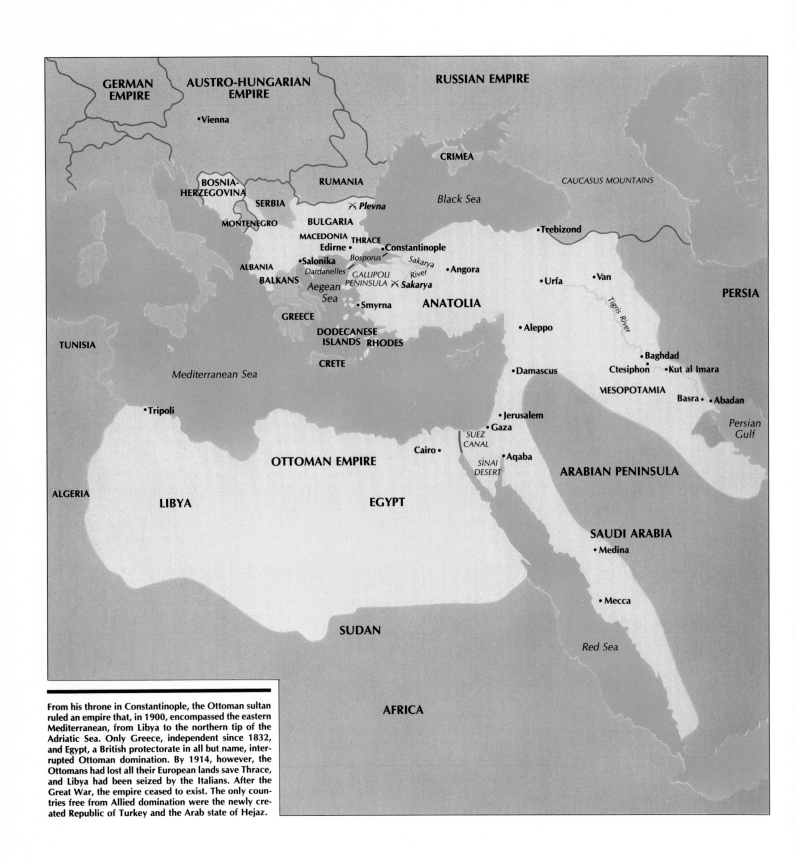

GERMAN EMPIRE

AUSTRO-HUNGARIAN EMPIRE

•Vienna

RUSSIAN EMPIRE

CRIMEA

CAUCASUS MOUNTAINS

Black Sea

BOSNIA-HERZEGOVINA

RUMANIA

SERBIA

⚔ Plevna

MONTENEGRO

BULGARIA

•Trebizond

MACEDONIA   THRACE

Edirne •

•Constantinople

Sakarya

•Salonika

Bosporus

River

•Angora

ALBANIA

Dardanelles

GALLIPOLI
PENINSULA

⚔ Sakarya

•Urfa

•Van

PERSIA

BALKANS

Aegean
Sea

ANATOLIA

•Smyrna

GREECE

•Aleppo

Tigris River

DODECANESE
ISLANDS   RHODES

•Baghdad

TUNISIA

CRETE

Mediterranean Sea

•Damascus

Ctesiphon

•Kut al Imara

MESOPOTAMIA

Basra •

•Abadan

•Tripoli

•Jerusalem

•Gaza

Persian
Gulf

Cairo •

SUEZ
CANAL

•Aqaba

ALGERIA

OTTOMAN EMPIRE

SINAI
DESERT

ARABIAN PENINSULA

LIBYA

EGYPT

SAUDI ARABIA

• Medina

SUDAN

• Mecca

AFRICA

Red Sea

From his throne in Constantinople, the Ottoman sultan ruled an empire that, in 1900, encompassed the eastern Mediterranean, from Libya to the northern tip of the Adriatic Sea. Only Greece, independent since 1832, and Egypt, a British protectorate in all but name, interrupted Ottoman domination. By 1914, however, the Ottomans had lost all their European lands save Thrace, and Libya had been seized by the Italians. After the Great War, the empire ceased to exist. The only countries free from Allied domination were the newly created Republic of Turkey and the Arab state of Hejaz.

Austria. The Black Sea was an Ottoman lake, and Ottoman territory stretched down along the coasts of the Red Sea and the Persian Gulf on either side of the Arabian Peninsula. The empire was made up of many races—Slav, Arab, Jew, Armenian, Kurd, and Greek; but at its center lay the the Anatolian peninsula, which was the homeland of the Ottoman Turks.

Anatolia nearly touches Europe across the narrow waters connecting the Black Sea with the Aegean. On the European side of this strategic waterway, where the Bosporus widens to become the Sea of Marmara, the city of Constantinople served as the opulent seat of the Ottoman sultans. It was from this teeming capital that the Ottoman government directed the fortunes of its subject peoples.

The power of the sultan was absolute, but it filtered slowly through an empire that was governed more as a mosaic of separate compartments than as a coherent whole. Theoretically, the state owned almost all of the agricultural land, and it collected a tax of between one-tenth and one-third of its produce. In practice, however, a large percentage of this revenue was granted to local notables who administered the countryside in the name of the sultan, supplying troops and weapons in times of war. Powerful trade guilds, which depended upon the Ottoman government for their status, performed a similar function in the towns. Accordingly, for most individuals, the diktats of Constantinople had little influence on the ordering of their day-to-day lives.

The sultan maintained only a tenuous hold over a population that in 1600 may have numbered as many as 30 million people. But, with the judicious application of military force, it was sufficient. The sultan, moreover, had God on his side: The vast majority of his subjects were Sunni Muslims, for whom the caliph—the temporal and spiritual successor of Muhammad— was a leader sanctified by religion. Since 1517, that title had been claimed by the sultan himself. Therefore, on the occasions when local grievances flared into open revolt, the uprising was more often directed against the provincial administrators than against the sultan.

By 1800, however, the Ottoman Empire was beginning to come apart. Defeated in a series of disastrous campaigns in the latter years of the seventeenth century, it had lost territory to Austria and Russia along its northern frontier. Even worse defeats had followed a century later, when Russia captured all Ottoman possessions on the northern coast of the Black Sea and extracted from the humiliated Ottomans the promise to allow the czar to protect Christian interests in Constantinople. The empire was on the defensive, its provinces rebellious, its army inefficient, and its bureaucracy corrupt. Europe was simply waiting for its imminent collapse.

But the "sick man of Europe," as Western leaders by now dismissively labeled the Ottoman realm, was not yet ready to die. In the early decades of the nineteenth century, the energetic sultan Mahmud II instituted a series of military and administrative reforms aimed at bringing the empire into parity with the West. Among the more visible signs of change was the abandonment of the traditional turban in favor of the businesslike red fez—which, being brimless, still allowed a devout Muslim to touch his forehead to the ground while at prayer.

The reforms, however, did little to prevent the continued erosion of Ottoman territory. In 1830, Algeria fell to the French; two years later, rebellious Christian subjects, aided by European powers, formed the independent kingdom of Greece; and by 1840, following ten years of unrest, Egypt had gained its own ruler and remained Ottoman in name only.

A remedy for the ailing empire did not come from Mahmud's successors, most of whom seemed to be more interested in their own pleasures than in politics. His son, Abdul Mejid, for example, expended his scant energy in planning the 300-room Dolmabache Palace, whose decorations alone consumed fourteen tons of gold leaf. Abdul Mejid's successor, Abdul Aziz, was distinguished principally for his gluttony and extravagance. Under his misrule, the Ottoman Empire accumulated a foreign debt of 200 million British pounds, while the sultan staged mock battles in the palace cellars or pursued chickens through the state chambers. But as the sultans frittered money away on extravagant caprices, a continuing process of reform was gradually strengthening Ottoman society. The earlier moves toward change were boosted in 1839 by the *Tanzimat* (literally, "regulations"), a series of reforms that were initiated by imperial administrators and that aimed to both modernize the empire and consolidate it under central government. Conscription was introduced to create a large standing army of approximately 300,000 men, which was used not only for war but also for maintaining internal order; provincial government was overhauled; a comprehensive system of state education was set up to provide a new breed of officers and bureaucrats; and new laws were promulgated that were to be applicable to all imperial subjects.

For some people, however, the changes were not enough, and there emerged an underground political movement that was to have a profound effect on the future of the empire. The Society of New Ottomans, though officially banned, grew from a tiny secret organization in the 1860s to an influential movement that had sympathizers throughout the empire. Among its supporters were many who believed that the sultan's monopoly of power contravened Muslim theology. Traditional Islamic thinking, they noted, espoused equality among all people, and advocated a representative assembly to check the unbridled power of rulers. Other supporters, mostly bureaucrats who had some knowledge of Western ideas, called for a greater liberalism along secular European lines. Whatever their differences, the members of the Society of New Ottomans were united in the belief that the empire could survive only by controlling the extravagances of its rulers and by adopting a constitution with provisions for a representative assembly.

The opportunity for change occurred in 1876. Having borrowed huge amounts from the West to pay for the costs of reform (and also to subsidize the sultans' grandiose whims), the empire was now bankrupt, unable to pay even the interest on its debt. Enraged by this default, Europeans demanded action. Their financial pique turned to righteous indignation when journalists reported the brutal suppression by Ottoman troops of a popular rebellion in Bulgaria. Centuries of Christian resentment now erupted into violent hatred of the Turks—the "great antihuman specimen of humanity," as the English statesman William Gladstone apoplectically described them. With Christian lives—as well as Christian money—in danger, it was obvious to Western bankers and humanitarians alike that the Ottoman Empire could not continue under its present regime. Consequently, a conference was called in Constantinople, where delegates from all the European powers gathered to settle the so-called Eastern Question.

At this crucial juncture, the Ottoman liberals, led by a former governor of Bulgaria named Midhat Pasha, took matters into their own hands. They forced the sultan Abdul Aziz to resign. He died mysteriously five days later. His nephew Murad—a feeble-minded alcoholic who was declared incurably insane by a Viennese specialist—served as sultan for only three months before he, too, was asked to step down. The next in line was Murad's brother, Abdul Hamid.

Before assuming power, this wily ruler had secretly agreed with the reformers to adopt a constitution guaranteeing equal rights to all Ottoman citizens. With impeccable timing, the revolution in state policy was announced on the first day of the conference. "In the presence of this great event, I feel that our task is superfluous," announced the Ottoman representative, scarcely concealing his satisfaction. With little left to debate, the conference collapsed after only a few days, giving the empire a new lease on life.

A portrait of Enver Bey reveals the ambitious self-confidence that thrust the twenty-seven-year-old officer to the forefront of the Young Turk Revolution that seized power in Istanbul in 1908. A flamboyant and charismatic leader, Enver was a prominent figure in the Army of Deliverance that marched on Istanbul in 1909 to protect the new constitutional government from a threatened counterrevolution and to depose the sultan. A spell as military attaché in Berlin fostered the pro-German tendencies that led him, as minister of war in 1914, to ally the Ottoman Empire with Germany.

Anyone believing that the Ottoman Empire was on the verge of becoming a constitutional monarchy was, however, quickly disillusioned. Abdul Hamid II was a ruthless despot who made concessions to modernization only to strengthen his own position. Within two years of his accession, the new sultan was confident enough to suspend the British-style parliament that had optimistically assembled in 1877, and to exile the one liberal leader that might have posed a threat to his regime: Midhat Pasha, who was the architect of the reform movement. There was little protest. Many Ottoman citizens retained a great sense of loyalty to their ruler's ancient dynasty and saw Abdul Hamid's despotic leadership as a step toward regaining the empire's lost glory.

In this they were overly optimistic: The empire was once again struggling for survival. The Balkan provinces of Bosnia and Herzegovina (today part of Yugoslavia) had been misruled and exploited for generations and were now ablaze with rebellion. The Western powers suggested a negotiated settlement, but Abdul Hamid haughtily declined their assistance. This was the moment Russia had long been waiting for. Claiming to act in the interest of Christianity in the Balkan States, the czar declared war on the Ottoman Empire in 1877. If Constantinople and control of the Bosporus should fall into Russian hands, so much the better.

The war lasted barely nine months. Despite a heroic stand at the Bulgarian village of Plevna—which the Russian grand duke, Nicholas, described as "one of the most splendid military feats in history"—the sultan's forces were steadily driven back by the larger, better-equipped Russian army. By January 1878, with the Russians only sixty miles from Constantinople, the Turks surrendered. However bitter their defeat, they could take some comfort in knowing that they had won the propaganda war. The defense of Plevna had captured popular European sympathy in a way that would have seemed inconceivable just two years earlier. From brutal murderers of helpless Christians, the Ottomans had become—temporarily at least—gallant underdogs fighting off the imperialist Russian bully. Plevna also proved that fifty years of military reform had borne fruit. The Turkish army revealed itself as a tenacious fighting force, a fact confirmed by the events of the next few decades.

In spite of its comprehensive defeat, the empire lost less territory than might have been expected. Russia, it is true, at first forced Constantinople to accept extraordinarily harsh terms in the Treaty of San Stefano of 1878. But the other European powers refused to stand by while the czar redrew the map of southeastern Europe to his own advantage, and they intervened to demand a renegotiation of the peace settlement. At the Congress of Berlin later that year, Rumania, Serbia, and Montenegro gained their independence from the Ottomans, and Austria assumed control of both Bosnia and Herzegovina. Cyprus passed into British hands and Bulgaria became an autonomous state. Russia made extensive gains in Asia and took southern Bessarabia from Rumania—which was subsequently compensated with Ottoman territory. to the south—but the Russians were not satisfied. "We have sacrificed a hundred thousand picked soldiers and a hundred million of money for nothing," remarked one disillusioned Russian general.

While the Ottomans lost ground in the Balkans through warfare, a chance to recover power in Egypt was missed through mismanagement and neglect. Since the completion of the Suez Canal in 1869, Egypt had become a focus of attention for the European powers, especially Britain, which began to regard this vital link with its Indian possessions as its own waterway. When a new military government with an Islamic and defiantly antiforeign attitude seized power in Cairo, Britain urged Abdul Hamid to join it in suppressing the rebellion. Although a joint expedition would have reinstated Constantinople's declining influence in this region, the superstitious sultan, on the advice of his astrologer, declined to make a decision. In 1882, Britain moved in alone, easily crushing the rebel government and effectively making the country a British protectorate.

As if reflecting the disintegrating state over which he ruled, Abdul Hamid himself grew increasingly unstable. At his best he was an energetic and clever politician, whose great achievement was to convince Muslims worldwide that the Ottoman cause was theirs. To this end he emphasized his role as the caliph, stressed popular Islam in the press, patronized the mystical Sufi orders, and supported the construction of the Hejaz railway for pilgrims who were traveling from Damascus to Medina. On the negative side, the sultan was paranoid, unpredictable, and cruel. Obsessed by the fear of assassination, he employed a dreaded network of spies, whose reports he received in Yildiz, the fortified estate built to his own design, within whose walls he spent most of his life. All his food was prepared behind the barred windows of a secure kitchen, and even then it had to be tasted by the Guardian of the Sultan's Health and Life and often a pet or two before it could pass Abdul Hamid's lips. One thousand loaded revolvers lay concealed in Yildiz; the sultan knew their whereabouts as well as how to use them.

This gaunt, unhappy man—who feared that even his clothing might be poisoned—nursed a particular dread of the exiled Midhat Pasha. Cabling to Midhat that "all was forgiven" and that his country needed him, Abdul Hamid lured his enemy back to

Bulgarian troops advance along a mountain road toward the Serbian frontier in 1913, during the Second Balkan War. The year before, in 1912, Serbia and Bulgaria had allied with Greece and Montenegro to defeat the Ottomans in the First Balkan War. The victors fought over the spoils, however, and in the ensuing renewed hostilities, the Ottoman Empire was able to regain some of the territory lost in the earlier conflict.

Constantinople, then immediately arrested him for the murder of the sultan Abdul Aziz. The trial was no more than a formality, the verdict a foregone conclusion. Prevented from cross-examining government witnesses, Midhat was found guilty and sentenced to exile in Arabia, where he was later strangled. Constantinople rumormongers claimed that his embalmed head was sent to Abdul Hamid in a case marked "Japanese ivories." It was not long after the murder of Midhat that Abdul Hamid became known as Abdul the Damned.

One community above all others in his heterogeneous realm bore the burden of the ruler's suspicions. Scattered throughout Anatolia, but concentrated especially in its mountainous eastern region, lived the Armenians, a devoutly Christian people who had long existed in peace with their Muslim overlords. Infected by the spirit of nationalism that was sweeping many parts of the Ottoman Empire, a minority of Armenians had allied themselves with the Russians during the war of 1877 in the hopes of establishing an independent state. Since then, supported by a number of influential expatriates in Europe and the United States, they had increasingly expressed their discontent through acts of terrorism.

To Abdul Hamid, there was only one way of dealing with what he saw as a race of dissidents: to kill them. Accordingly, over a period of three years, from 1894 to 1896, Armenian men, women, and children alike were massacred. Although Ottoman troops played a role in this pogrom, much of the slaughter was carried out by local Muslims and neighboring Kurdish tribes. In the southern city of Urfa, in just one instance of the terror, 3,000 Armenians sought sanctuary in the cathedral, where they were burned alive by a mob.

In spite of Abdul Hamid's efforts to suppress news of the massacres—Turkish newspapers were prohibited from even using the word "Armenian"—Europe and Russia inevitably became aware of the attempted genocide. Although Britain repeatedly called for concerted action, nothing happened until terrorism and rioting in the streets of Constantinople threatened foreign business communities and the peace of their embassies. Abdul Hamid was then urged to desist from policies that "would imperil both the sultan's throne and his dynasty." For more than 100,000 Armenians, this strongly worded telegram was dispatched too late.

Although there was widespread condemnation in the West, the Ottomans did gain one friend among the European nations. Germany became an outspoken supporter of the unloved sultan, extending credit to the bankrupt empire in return for business favors. As Britain, France, and Russia watched apprehensively, German concessionaries slowly started to realize a plan cherished by their ruler, Kaiser Wilhelm, to build a railway linking Berlin with Baghdad. A German military mission also exerted a steady influence upon the Ottoman army. The kaiser even visited Constantinople in 1898 to assure Abdul Hamid of his support.

Friends at home were becoming harder to find. As Abdul Hamid's reign wore on, it became clear that he did, indeed, have cause to fear for his life. In 1904, a knife-wielding officer attacked him within the walls of Yildiz; the following year, he was nearly killed at prayer by a load of dynamite planted outside Constantinople's Hamidieh Mosque. (Such were his fears of assassination by now that the sultan forbade anyone standing near him to put his hand in his pocket.) These dramatic incidents reflected a growing unrest within Turkish society. A large number of dissidents had already fled to Europe, where they circulated radical literature and plotted the downfall of the regime. Abdul Hamid's own brother-in-law was among them. "Your Majesty's mode of government conforms to no law," Mahmud Pasha rebuked the sultan from the safety of Paris.

Other subversives remained at home. Under the most intense secrecy, they gradually infiltrated all professions, as well as all branches of the bureaucracy and the military. Even Abdul Hamid's own secret police eventually included agents of these Young Turks, as the clandestine reformers became known. Their aims were not truly revolutionary; most wanted to strengthen the empire, not overturn it. It was only the fear of bloody purges that kept these loosely linked organizations underground. The group of medical students who formed the Ottoman Union in 1889, for instance, were principally interested in reinstating the constitution of 1876, and particularly in reconvening the elected assembly that Abdul Hamid had suspended early in his reign. Over the next twenty years, this group merged with others, eventually forming the Committee of Union and Progress, or CUP—letters that were to spell an end to the Hamidian era.

The overthrow of Abdul Hamid, when it finally occurred, surprised both ruler and rebels with its swiftness. By 1908, the CUP had a strong following in Macedonia, a rebellious and multiracial province bordering on Greece. Salonika, the capital of Macedonia, was a center of antigovernment activity, and it was there, in May, that Abdul Hamid sent a commission to investigate reports of sedition within the military. Acting as much from fear of discovery and retribution as from any preplanned schedule for revolution, dissident army officers in the province rebelled. Within two months, the armed forces of the region were in full revolt and were threatening to march on Constantinople if the sultan did not honor the constitution. On July 23, taking advice once again from his astrologer, Abdul Hamid meekly acquiesced to the demands of the rebels.

The populace of Constantinople reacted to this news with astonishment and delight. Suddenly their newspapers were openly discussing "freedom" and an "elected assembly," concepts that could not have been safely whispered just a day before. Bulgarians and Greeks, Armenians and Turks embraced one another in the streets. Ironically, Abdul Hamid was accorded much of the credit for this new day; cruelly misled by his councilors, it was argued, he had courageously accepted the need for change. Thousands flocked to Yildiz, where their surprised ruler, now a mere constitutional monarch, greeted them from his balcony.

What pique the Young Turks might have felt at this popular support for Abdul Hamid was soon forgotten in the face of a more immediate threat. In 1909, envious army officers, resentful of the success of their rebellious colleagues, staged a countercoup that found support among fundamentalist Muslims. The revolt was quickly suppressed, but the

Antipodean members of the Allied forces crowd a sea front on the Gallipoli Peninsula in 1915. The narrow, enclosed beach at Anzac Cove—acronymically named after the Australian and New Zealand Army Corps that landed there—offered little space for stores, so makeshift huts and dugouts were set up on the hillside. Soldiers were at the front as soon as they landed: The shelters on the hillside were generally no more than 100 feet from the Allied trenches. Hemmed in by the terrain and the enemy, the Anzacs remained helplessly pinioned until their evacuation in December 1915.

THE ARAB REVOLT

"Tall, graceful, vigorous" was Lawrence's description of Faisal, borne out in this portrait of March 1917. A popular leader, Faisal overcame tribal factionalism to unite the Arabs against the Ottomans.

An Arab headdress contrasts with the British uniform of T. E. Lawrence. Lawrence earned the nickname Emir Dynamite for his daring raids behind Ottoman lines.

On June 10, 1916, Sharif Husayn, Arab ruler of the Red Sea province of Hejaz, leaned from his balcony in Mecca and fired a rifle shot at the nearby Ottoman barracks. The gesture symbolized years of frustrated Arab nationalism, and within weeks, an armed revolt, spearheaded by Husayn's son, Emir Faisal, was gaining force. The British, eager to exploit the threat to the Ottomans, offered military help as well as the prospect of a favorable settlement for the Arabs at the end of the world war. Among others, a young officer named T. E. Lawrence was sent as a liaison between Faisal and the British army.

Leaving the city of Medina under siege, an Arab army moved north, harassing the Ottomans with guerrilla hit-and-run tactics, then taking the port of Aqaba, 800 miles from Mecca, in July 1917. Under the inspired leadership of Faisal and Lawrence, the army inched its way toward Damascus, joining with the British to capture this Ottoman stronghold on October 1, 1918.

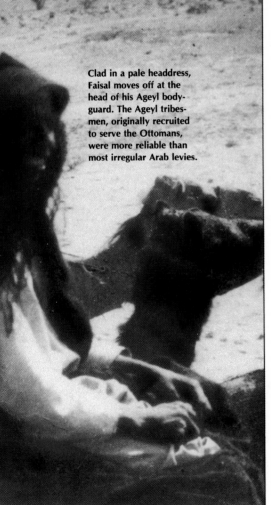

Clad in a pale headdress, Faisal moves off at the head of his Ageyl bodyguard. The Ageyl tribesmen, originally recruited to serve the Ottomans, were more reliable than most irregular Arab levies.

Young Turks now took steps to secure their hold on the foundering state. They amended the constitution to give the assembly increased power, and they demoted the sultan to a figurehead.

Unwilling to take any risks, the National Assembly determined to go one step further and depose Abdul Hamid. On April 29, 1909, four elected representatives called on the sultan and informed him of the new government's decision. "It is kismet (fate). I am not guilty," said the sultan.

It only remained to deport Abdul Hamid to Salonika and dismantle the ostentatious trappings of his rule. From the halls of Yildiz came sacks of gold, four dozen grand pianos, and thousands of shirts, some with jewels lying forgotten in their pockets. Now, too, the harem was disbanded.

Abdul Hamid, still with a substantial retinue of wives, concubines, servants, and eunuchs, was later to return to Constantinople, where he died peacefully in 1918. Meanwhile his brother, who confessed to not having read a newspaper in twenty years, became Mehmed V, a sultan only in name.

Real power now resided with the Young Turks, chiefly members of the CUP and radical military officers who had contributed to Abdul Hamid's fall. Conspicuous among this new breed of politicians were Enver Bey and Talaat Bey. Enver, a dashing young officer, was handsome, fearless, charming, and as events were to prove, as cruel as any sultan. Born into poverty, he eventually realized his longing for luxury by marrying one of Abdul Hamid's daughters and living in a palace. Talaat, once a humble employee of the post office, rose to become minister of the interior. A powerful man with "a huge sweeping back and rocky biceps," as the American ambassador recalled, he was the driving force of the CUP. These men and their colleagues, though inexperienced in governing, attempted to speed up the process of technical modernization and social reform, believing that these policies alone could save the empire from collapse. They were to preside over one of the most disastrous decades of Ottoman history.

Constantinople's novice government was not granted any favors by its European neighbors. The Young Turks had scarcely seized power when Austria completed its annexation of Bosnia, which it had administered since 1878. Simultaneously, Bulgaria declared its independence and Greece peacefully assumed control of the island of Crete. In the meantime, Italy, which was seeking a colony of its own on the North African coast, had been building up its economic interests in Tripoli. To facilitate matters, the Italian government abruptly declared war in 1911. Local Arab armies put up a spirited resistance to this unprovoked attack, but Italy won its modest prize after a year of fighting. It added to the spoils of war by seizing Rhodes and the Dodecanese Islands as well, promising to give them back when the Ottomans formally surrendered Tripoli. In the confusion of the years that followed, this promise was conveniently forgotten.

Ottoman territory in Europe had been reduced by now to Macedonia, Albania, and Thrace, the eastern tip of the Balkans that included Constantinople. The newly independent Balkan States, which looked upon these lands as natural extensions of their own domains, saw Constantinople's preoccupation with North Africa as an opportunity not to be missed. In 1912, Bulgaria, Serbia, Greece, and Montenegro, acting with rare accord, swept into Ottoman territory. Within two months, Macedonia had fallen; worse still, the Bulgarians were poised in Thrace to take Edirne, ancient residence of the Ottoman sultans, and had advanced to within twenty miles of Constantinople itself.

Just as the Ottoman government was preparing to surrender all the occupied lands, Enver Bey, who had seen action in both North Africa and the Balkans, staged a flamboyant coup d'état. To cries of "We will hold Edirne," the pistol-waving Enver and his fellow rebels burst into the government's council chamber, assassinated the minister of war, and cut short all peace negotiations. Now in sole command of the armed forces, Enver dismissed 1,200 officers in a single day and resumed the war. The Bulgarians promptly bombarded Edirne into submission and moved deeper into eastern Thrace, where they embarked upon a campaign of slaughter against the Turkish peasantry. In the spring of 1913, a humbled Enver was forced to sue for peace. The First Balkan War was at an end.

The peace was short-lived. Within a month of their victory, the triumphant Balkan allies—never the best of neighbors—began to fight among themselves. Suddenly Bulgaria found itself at war with Greece, Serbia, and from the north, Rumania. The conflict was particularly savage. "We are told of human beings saturated with oil and set on fire," wrote a contemporary historian about the Second Balkan War, "of persons buried to the neck and abandoned to a slow death with basins of food and water before their eyes."

In the midst of this carnage, Ottoman troops easily drove the beleaguered Bulgarians from Edirne and then recaptured eastern Thrace. But the land was scarcely worth possessing. "The country looks as if it had been swept by a terrible earthquake," observed the first Western reporter on the scene, adding naively, "It is almost impossible to believe one is living in the twentieth century with such evidence of man's ferocity all around."

On his return from this wasteland, Enver Bey was greeted as a hero and was awarded the honorific title of Pasha. In the flush of unexpected victory, it was easy to forget that in two years the Ottomans had lost 80 percent of their European territory. The memory of the two Balkan wars—whether of triumph or defeat—was soon to fade, however, because just five years later, the Ottoman Empire itself would be no more than a memory.

In 1914, as the edifice of European diplomacy crumbled into war, it was uncertain which side the Ottomans would choose. Overtures had already been made to Britain and France, but finally, looking for protection against Russia, Enver Pasha—now minister of war—had formed a secret alliance with Germany. Nevertheless, Talaat Bey spoke for the majority of his compatriots when he insisted to Enver, "We want nothing more than to be left out of the war." Within two months, public opinion had shifted. When Britain commandeered two warships it had built for the Ottoman navy, there was widespread resentment. It seemed only natural, therefore, that the Ottomans should give refuge to two fleeing German warships, the *Goeben* and *Breslau*, and incorporate them into their navy. When these ships, manned by a fez-wearing German crew, sailed through the Bosporus to bombard Russian ports in the Black Sea, the empire's entry into the war was inevitable.

Few Western politicians had anticipated that the Middle East would play an important part in the war. The Allied powers of Britain, France, and Russia had made little effort to woo the empire, because they did not expect it to be a significant factor in the fighting. They were cruelly mistaken.

One of the Ottomans' first actions was to proclaim a jihad, or "holy war," against

LIFELINES THROUGH THE DESERT

In sweltering heat, British soldiers position some of the 50,000 rolls of wire netting used in crossing the desert. The mesh provided a firm surface on which to tread, doubling the troops' speed.

Local Egyptian laborers stand beside a section of twelve-inch pipe. When it was completed, the pipeline carried drinking water 300 miles from the Nile to the Palestinian border.

Finishing touches are applied to a section of railway. By 1917, the Allies had constructed more than 350 miles of track to provide troops with supplies and equipment.

Combined Ottoman and German attacks on the strategic Suez Canal spurred the Allies to take retaliatory measures in 1916. To reach the enemy bases in Palestine, however, they first had to cross the sunscorched inhospitable wastes of the Sinai.

A camel corps was created to form the vanguard of the Allied supply train. Comprising about 34,000 mounts of eight different breeds, it was not without its problems. Standardizing equipment for the animals was hard, and the creatures were not particularly tractable: In one year, seventy men lost limbs from camel bites.

Behind the camels, a well-organized trail of ordnance moved along a hastily built road-and-rail network. Wire netting was laid to ease the marching, and piping was imported from the United States to supply the troops with fresh water. Eleven months' hard toil was vindicated in March 1917, when the Allies finally reached the Palestinian town of Gaza.

the empire's infidel foes, with the intention of spreading disaffection among Muslims in Allied territories. Although this caused alarm, particularly in Britain, whose empire contained a large Muslim population, few non-Ottomans responded. But this did not prevent Ottoman forces from marching against the Russians in the Caucasus, hoping to incite an uprising among local Muslim tribesmen. The looked-for rebellion never materialized, and by January 1915, Ottoman forces were suffering terrible losses. This costly eastern campaign, which lasted for more than two years, at one point tied down half the Ottoman army, seriously reducing the empire's ability to wage war on other fronts. It also brought the Ottomans into another bloody confrontation with the Armenians of eastern Anatolia.

A mixed force of Russians and Armenian guerrillas had reached the city of Van on May 14 and had begun to massacre the local Muslim population, at the same time declaring an independent Armenian state. Armenians flocked to Van from all directions; indeed, by mid-July, the region's population had increased by an estimated 500 percent. That month, however, an Ottoman counteroffensive drove back the Russians, along with thousands of refugees from the short-lived Armenian state. Up to 40,000 people died from exposure, disease, and starvation during this flight. Those who remained fared no better. Inflamed by the jihad, and furious at the apparent perfidy of the Armenians, local officials and troops acted with the utmost savagery, butchering the men, then robbing and raping the women before leaving them to die. In the city of Van alone, an American medical missionary reported that there were 55,000 Armenian deaths.

The official government policy was to deport the Armenian population to less volatile western areas. Some such movements existed only on paper. When one conscientious officer asked Talaat Bey where he was supposed to send a convoy of Armenians, he received a chilling reply: "The place they are being sent to is nowhere." Those convoys that did set out were hardly more fortunate. Of 18,000 Armenians who journeyed across the desert to Aleppo on one expedition, only 150 survived the depredations of their guards and local tribesmen to reach their destination. Half a million or more Armenians died as a result of this brutal policy. Many more fled to the Caucasus. "I have accomplished more toward solving the Armenian problem in three months than Abdul Hamid accomplished in thirty years," Talaat Bey was said to have boasted.

If events on their eastern front won the Ottoman troops no great glory, their heroic performance in the west was to astonish the Allies. Late in 1914, Winston Churchill, Britain's first lord of the Admiralty, had expressed his discontent at the shape that the war in Europe was taking. "Are there not other alternatives than sending our armies to chew barbed wire in Flanders?" he complained. The alternative he proposed was an assault on Constantinople from the Aegean Sea via the Dardanelles. It was an imaginative plan that very nearly succeeded in its earliest stages. In February 1915, a British naval bombardment silenced the Ottoman guns on the Anatolian side of the strait. The defending troops were out of ammunition and on the point of surrendering when the British, unaware of their enemy's condition, suddenly abandoned the attack. They prepared instead to seize the strategic Gallipoli Peninsula on the other side of the Dardanelles.

In the spring and summer of 1915, British, Australian, and New Zealand troops made several attempts to capture the barren plateau of Gallipoli. Their maps were inadequate and their coordination at times was poor. In addition to these drawbacks, they met with a German-trained Ottoman army that was defending the very heart of the empire. Time and again the invading forces struggled up the heights of the peninsula only to be beaten back by Ottoman soldiers who willingly fought to the death rather than give ground.

Commanding the defense, and seemingly immune to the bullets, was a headstrong and inspirational young colonel named Mustafa Kemal. Born in the Macedonian town of Salonika in 1881, he was the son of a timber merchant whose business had been ruined by Greek brigands; Kemal had graduated from the prestigious Ottoman

The British commander, General Allenby, backed by Allied officers and local notables, stands by the British military governor as he reads the proclamation of occupation before Jerusalem's ancient citadel. Jerusalem was not of great strategic significance during the world war, but because it was a holy center for Jews, Christians, and Muslims alike, its capture from the Ottomans held symbolic importance. Following the city's surrender without a struggle, Allenby showed respect for its religious status: When he officially entered the city on December 11, 1917, he did so on foot rather than by car or on horseback.

Staff College in 1905, gaining valuable military experience against the Italian invaders of Libya in 1912. Now he had taken on the defense of Gallipoli as a personal crusade. He infected his men with the same spirit. "I am not ordering you to attack, I am ordering you to die," he instructed his officers. "In the time it takes us to die, other forces can come and take our place."

Throughout nine months' fighting, the Ottomans clung grimly to their positions, constantly bringing Allied attacks to a halt. Only massive reinforcements could have broken the stalemate, and these the Allies simply did not have. After having suffered some 214,000 casualties—twice those of the Ottomans—the Allies withdrew, and in

Flanked by British military and diplomatic officials, Emir Faisal remains seated during his installation in Baghdad as king of Iraq on August 23, 1921. Briefly king of Syria following the war, Faisal was ejected by the French after the area fell under their mandate in 1920. The next year, Great Britain sponsored him as king of their own mandate in Iraq, realizing that it would relieve them of many of their administrative problems if the Iraqis were to accept this popular Pan-Arab leader as their ruler.

January 1916, the Gallipoli campaign came to an end. General Liman von Sanders, a German officer employed by the Ottomans, later confessed that only Mustafa Kemal's dogged resistance kept his divisional generals from ordering a withdrawal. The Savior of the Dardanelles, as Kemal was hailed on his return to Constantinople, was hastily reassigned to the eastern front by an envious Enver Pasha, who detested the intense young colonel.

The high drama of the Dardanelles was not repeated on other fronts, where the Allies, represented mainly by Great Britain, gradually exhausted the Ottoman Empire's capacity to defend itself. In so doing, however, the British were forced to commit large numbers of men to the Middle East, troops that might otherwise have shortened the war in Europe.

In Mesopotamia, present-day Iraq, the British advanced from the Persian Gulf along the course of the Tigris River toward Baghdad. After an easy victory at Basra near the coast, they were repulsed by Ottoman forces at Ctesiphon, then driven back to Kut al Imara, where they were forced to surrender. The British renewed their efforts, with the result that Baghdad was seized early in 1917. The justification for this costly expedition was not entirely clear. Critics claimed that the capture of Baghdad was as much a means of saving face after the Gallipoli debacle as of achieving any strategic advantage.

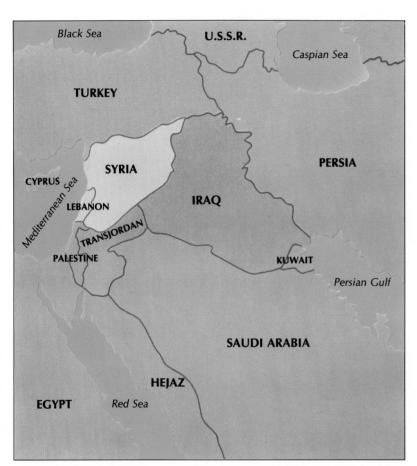

After the Ottoman surrender in 1918, the empire's former territories in the Middle East were divided between the British and French, to be temporarily administered under League of Nations mandate. The Treaty of San Remo, on April 24, 1920, gave Syria and Lebanon *(shaded yellow on the map)* to the French; Iraq, Palestine, and Transjordan *(shaded orange)* were placed in the British sphere. Iraq gained independence in 1930, but the two Western powers continued to control the other mandates until the Second World War.

In Egypt, the Ottomans boldly attacked Great Britain's positions on the Suez Canal; nevertheless, they were driven back across the Sinai Desert into Palestine. British forces pursued them, painstakingly advancing toward the city of Jerusalem, which they captured in the latter part of 1917.

It was at this point that the British foreign secretary, Lord Balfour, issued a remarkable statement promising that Britain would encourage the establishment in Palestine of "a national home for the Jewish people," as long as this did nothing to prejudice the civil and religious rights of the existing Palestinians. By this act, he partly endorsed the goal of the Zionist movement, which had been agitating for the creation of a Jewish homeland since 1897; to this end, Zionist leaders had entered into negotiations with the Ottomans at the turn of the century. Although the talks proved counterproductive, Jewish settlers—including a long-established urban community—were forming an influential minority group in the region. Balfour stated that he was merely trying to win support for the Allies from powerful Jewish groups in Russia as well as in the United States. Some people claimed that he was inspired by a genuine sympathy for the Zionist cause; others said that Britain was simply attempting to strengthen its claim to future control of the region for strategic reasons. Whatever Great Britain's motives—and it was likely that they were mixed—the Balfour Declaration had no discernible effect on the world war, although it was fraught with consequences for subsequent developments in the area.

While promising Jews a homeland in Palestine, the British were simultaneously urging the Arabs to throw off Ottoman rule and create their own independent states, to which end they sent arms and money to a leading notable of Mecca, Sharif Husayn. A northern army set up under his son, Emir Faisal, succeeded in destroying the Hejaz railway that linked Damascus and the Ottoman garrison in Medina. By 1917, the emir's army had taken Aqaba, linking Arab rebel territory with British forces in southern Palestine.

The relatively small amount of bloodshed in the desert war stood in stark contrast

BLOODBATH IN SMYRNA

A pall of smoke rises from Smyrna as fire consumes the Greek and Armenian quarters. Allied warships, forbidden to interfere in Turkish domestic affairs, at first would not accept refugees, but they later reversed their orders in response to the fire.

Clutching whatever could be salvaged from their homes in the city or the devastated countryside, Greeks and other foreigners line up on the harbor front at Smyrna, awaiting evacuation.

Cheering Turks crowd around a huge victory flag made especially to celebrate the triumph at Smyrna. The Turkish quarter was one of the few areas of the city to be left untouched by the fire.

From the moment that Greek forces landed at the port of Smyrna on May 15, 1919, intent on colonizing western Anatolia in the wake of the Ottoman defeat in the Great War, Turkish nationalists waged a ferocious campaign to drive back the invaders. After three years of bloody fighting, Turkish troops recaptured Smyrna on September 9, 1922. But the liberation of Anatolia had a tragic ending. According to Turkish accounts, the vanquished enemy set fire to the Greek and Armenian quarters in revenge for defeat. Foreign witnesses, however, insisted that the city was burned not by Greeks but by Turks seeking to cover traces of slaughter, rape, and looting.

Whatever the cause, half of Smyrna was razed, including the whole of the Armenian and Greek quarters. Thousands of civilians died in the blaze; others drowned while seeking to escape by swimming out to Allied warships in the harbor. The final death toll may have been as high as 100,000.

to the appalling suffering of troops and civilians alike in the other war zones. When it finally agreed to an armistice in the autumn of 1918, the Ottoman Empire was on the verge of collapse. About 325,000 soldiers had been killed in action; 240,000 had fallen to disease; and an estimated 1.5 million had deserted. Civilian losses were beyond calculation, and many of the survivors were starving. Even the wealthy struggled with a cost of living that had risen 2.5 thousand percent over the course of the war.

The CUP government resigned on October 13, 1918. Three weeks later, in the dead of night, Enver Pasha and Talaat Bey fled ignominiously from their homelands in a German torpedo boat. Enver died four years later in a cavalry charge against Communist forces in the Soviet Union. Talaat was assassinated in 1921 on a Berlin street by an Armenian student who had lost his entire family in eastern Anatolia.

Determined to punish the enemy who had declared a holy war against them, the Allied powers devised a peace settlement that would dismember the Ottoman Empire, leaving Anatolia looking like a jigsaw puzzle of conflicting zones of interest. Under the Treaty of Sèvres, an independent Armenia was to occupy much of the land in the east, while Greece, France, and Italy were to have spheres of influence in the west, with the Bosporus becoming an international zone.

Once again the Allies had underestimated the religious fervor and national pride of the Turks. They had also committed the foolish error of encouraging Greece to annex Thrace and to seize the Anatolian city of Smyrna, a rich and ancient port on the Aegean coast with a large Greek population. It soon became clear that the new colonists were bent on revenge against their traditional enemy. Greek atrocities against the Muslim people of Thrace and Smyrna did much to inflame Turkish nationalism. The Italian occupying forces, too, behaved with a callousness that did little to recommend Christian civilization.

The Turkish people were divided concerning the best course of action. Some hoped to shelter with the puppet sultan—now Mehmed VI—under the wing of the Allied powers. In central Anatolia, however, a substantial number of Ottoman troops remained to trouble the occupying forces. At the Allied powers' behest, the Ottoman government appointed a Turkish general to pacify the region. Incredibly, the choice fell upon the one person who was capable of uniting the nation against the government and the foreign powers that backed it. That person was the Savior of the Dardanelles, Mustafa Kemal.

Since the Gallipoli campaign, Kemal had served with distinction in both the Caucasus and Palestine, but he had never achieved the same public acclaim. An outspoken and passionate nationalist, he employed rhetoric too fierce and solutions too radical for many Turks. Now, however, his hour had arrived. Suddenly he found himself inspector of the Third Army, speaking as an official representative of the sultan. "Your sultan has sent me to help you," he persuaded his audiences, and his solution was always the same: "You the Turkish people must save yourselves before the Allied troops destroy us."

Within two months of his arrival, Mustafa Kemal was dismissed from his post for insubordination. He resigned from the army but refused to return west as he had been

War hero turned schoolteacher, Turkish president Mustafa Kemal demonstrates the Latin alphabet during a tour of the country. The abandonment of Arabic script in 1929 was part of Kemal's overall plan for modernization of the nation. The move simplified spelling and dramatically reduced illiteracy; it also served Kemal's aim of loosening the hold of orthodox Islam, since all religious texts were still in the old lettering.

ordered. "I shall stay in Anatolia until the nation has won its independence," was the defiant message he delivered to Constantinople.

The Allies now resorted to desperate measures. Alarmed by outbursts of violence throughout the country—including another massacre of the Armenians—they occupied Constantinople in the spring of 1920 and dismissed the pronationalist government. Mustafa Kemal was sentenced to death *in absentia*. Kemal's response was to call a Grand National Assembly of Turkey in the central town of Angora, which at the time was famous chiefly for the production of mohair but which subsequently became the capital of the nation.

"The Grand National Assembly is the true and sole representative of the nation," proclaimed Mustafa Kemal. But the next few months almost brought an end to the nationalist movement. Racked by internal dissension, Mustafa Kemal and his followers were also forced to fight on several fronts. They confronted Armenians in the east, French in the south, Greeks in the west, as well as a ragtag army fighting in the name of the sultan and numerous tribal and religious uprisings inspired by Constantinople's antinationalist proclamations. Mustafa Kemal enlisted a similarly heterogeneous force, which included socialists, Communists, and Islamic radicals. Soviet Russia increasingly contributed material assistance; however, Mustafa Kemal's own fanatical dedication to his cause provided the principal explanation for the survival of the nationalists.

It was at this crucial point in nationalist fortunes that the Allies prepared to implement the peace plan that would cut into the very heart of the former Ottoman Empire. The Treaty of Sèvres, said Mustafa Kemal, was "a sinister sentence of death" upon the Turkish nation. The Allied powers also committed the error of using Greece to subdue the nationalists. Officially the Greek army was in charge of restoring peace, but the Greeks made no secret of their colonial ambitions toward Anatolia.

The threat of their enemies imposing upon them the terms of a brutal treaty rallied the Turks to the side of Mustafa Kemal as no amount of rhetoric had done in the past. They were only just in time. The well-equipped Greek army pushed effortlessly northward in 1920, while Mustafa was still trying to clothe his new recruits. To accomplish this task, he enlisted the entire local population, insisting that "every dwelling without exception has to supply a kit consisting of a parcel of underwear, a pair of socks, and a pair of shoes." Soviet Russia and Italy provided military aid, and now even France began to accept that Mustafa Kemal was no mere rebel but a genuine national leader.

Like the Russians at Plevna and the British at Gallipoli, the Greeks soon discovered that they had engaged a formidable enemy. Late in the summer of 1921, Mustafa Kemal retreated to the Sakarya River. There, in the mountainous heart of western Anatolia, he fought the battle that broke the Greek advance. Over a sixty-mile-long front, for twenty-two days and twenty-two nights the battle raged. In this rugged terrain, Mustafa Kemal's tactics were to divide his army into individual units, each operating independently of its neighbors, so that the Turkish line of defense could not be broken. "There is no linear defense," explained Mustafa Kemal. "There is a surface defense, and the surface is the entire territory of the nation." Fighting for their lives and their country, the Turks wore down the larger Greek army, forcing it to retreat in disarray.

The following summer, his army reequipped, Mustafa Kemal personally launched an offensive. "Soldiers forward," he ordered. "Your goal is the Aegean." The Greeks scarcely attempted to resist. In September 1922, Turkish troops triumphantly entered the city of Smyrna.

With the fall of Smyrna, only the British continued to resist Mustafa Kemal's claims to national leadership. At one tense moment, British and Turkish armies faced each other at Chanak, on the Asiatic coast of the Dardanelles, with just a few yards between them. Both commanders acted with restraint, however, and diplomats finally defused the situation by persuading Greece to abandon Thrace.

Mustafa Kemal's last opponent on the road to total victory was the sixty-one-year-old sultan, Mehmed VI, who was still the official head of the Ottoman state. Deputies to the Grand National Assembly in Angora were by no means unanimous in their desire to end the sultanate, but Mustafa Kemal bullied and persuaded them to accept this decisive step in the revolution. "Considering my life in Constantinople to be in danger," wrote the sultan to the commander of the British forces, "I take refuge with the British government." On November 17, 1922, the old man departed on a British flagship, leaving his cousin to take over the post of caliph. Among the few belongings that he carried with him was a set of solid gold coffee cups. A telegram that was sent by an American impresario to the British embassy in Constantinople provided an ironic footnote to the ending of the 700-year-old dynasty: "Hippodrome New York could use wives of ex-sultan. Kindly put me in touch with party who could procure them." The last sultan—with his wives unsold—died in the Italian resort of San Remo four years later.

During these years of unrest and civil war, the Ottoman Empire as such had ceased to exist. By the Treaty of Sèvres the empire had been stripped of its Arab provinces, most of which were placed as mandates under the temporary administration of Britain and France. Brushing aside local defenders, the French occupied Damascus in 1920 and established the states of Syria and Lebanon. Under British mandate and an Arab administration, Jordan—or Transjordan, as it was then called—was launched on the road to independence. Emir Faisal, briefly ruler of Syria, became king of Iraq under British mandate, uniting his country as an independent member of the League of Nations in 1932. Most of Arabia retained its independence, and eventually the Saud family formed the kingdom of Saudi Arabia.

The tragedy of Palestine, which had fallen under British mandate, was already emerging. Although Arabs still outnumbered Jews by nearly ten to one, they were resentful of Zionist attempts to establish a homeland and suspicious of Britain's motives. Violence between Arabs and Zionists broke out as early as 1918, and more seriously in 1920. The pattern was established for years of unrest.

In the other mandates, too, trouble was brewing. Within five years of the French occupation, the Syrians had risen in revolt, demanding independence for Greater Syria. And in Lebanon, the country was split between Muslim nationalists calling for a union with Syria, and a large Christian population seeking its own self-determination. The unrest was put down by French troops, but the region continued to be troublesome for its Western administrators until they finally relinquished control during the Second World War.

Bereft of much of the land with which it had entered the century, the rump of the old Ottoman state emerged in 1923 as the Republic of Turkey. It retained eastern Thrace, but otherwise its borders were essentially those of Anatolia.

The early story of the Republic of Turkey is that of Mustafa Kemal, who served as president from 1923 until his death in 1938. Few leaders have ever shaped a nation as quickly and permanently as he. One of his first moves was to abolish the office of caliph in 1924. "Religion is like a heavy blanket that keeps the people of Turkey asleep," he explained.

Modernization was Mustafa Kemal's only faith, and by that he meant the wholesale adoption of Western culture and technology. He introduced Western calendars and clocks, adopted the metric system, and encouraged orchestras to play Western music. Banks were nationalized, and electricity was brought to remote rural areas, while traditional Muslim practices such as polygamy and begging were outlawed. Women's education was promoted, and voting rights were extended to all citizens. He even carried his revolution into the world of everyday dress by banning the fez. This reform created a sudden rush to buy brimmed European headgear of every description. Mustafa Kemal sported a panama. In country districts, peasants could be seen wearing bowlers, stetsons, and even bonnets. His request that women should abandon the veil, however, met with stiff conservative opposition.

Among Mustafa Kemal's most enthusiastic projects was the reinvention of the Turkish language. Aiming to purge the written language of foreign influence, he helped prepare a new twenty-nine-letter Latin alphabet to take the place of the old Arabic script, and he himself was among the first to use it. Wherever it was possible, foreign borrowings were dropped, and academics were obliged to scour ancient texts for native Turkish replacements—although nothing could be found to substitute for such modern coinings as *otomobil* or *fotograf*. In spite of the inevitable confusion caused by this revolution, the literacy rate increased dramatically during the years of Mustafa Kemal's rule.

The use of Turkish placenames was also enforced. Angora, Smyrna, and Constantinople were henceforth to be known as Ankara, Izmir, and Istanbul. Eventually, even the Turkish people were forced to change their names. In 1934, traditional Arabic titles such as Pasha and Bey were abolished. Moreover, every man was obliged to adopt a surname in the Western fashion, rather than calling himself after his birthplace or profession. Mustafa Kemal hit upon the name of Atatürk, meaning "father of the Turk."

Critics of Kemal Atatürk—as he now called himself—remarked that, "You cannot make a Turk into a Westerner by giving him a hat." And it was true that new headgear, new names, and a new alphabet could not change centuries of custom overnight. In the early 1930s, more than 75 percent of the population was still engaged in agricultural work of some description, and the average peasant, lacking the capital, technology, or education to do otherwise, continued to scratch a living from some ten acres or less. The small villages built of mud and timber, centered on a mosque and a school, remained relatively self-contained, with the inhabitants building their own houses, keeping the village accounts, and running their own local courts. In many areas, transport depended on the peasants' heavy, wooden, rough-terrain carts, and medical knowledge was often rudimentary. Some country dwellers still considered ground crab to be an effective cure for consumption—perhaps one reason for an infant mortality rate that in some areas, according to one traveler in 1928, stood as high as 78 percent. But, thanks to Atatürk, changes in all these areas could now begin.

During his fifteen years as president, Kemal Atatürk governed Turkey with all the power and hauteur of a sultan. Indeed, his style had always resembled that of a despot. No one could challenge his passionate love for the Turkish people or his efforts to improve their lot, but he bitterly resented criticism and suppressed insurgents in a manner reminiscent of Abdul Hamid. (One Western traveler reported that ten men were killed for refusing to wear a hat.) He even moved into the Dolmabache, vast palace of the sultans. It was there that he died on November 10, 1938. He was mourned extravagantly, but genuinely, by his compatriots.

"The Turkish homeland has lost its great creator," lamented the official announcement of his death, "the Turkish nation a mighty chief, and humanity a great son." The modern Middle East, the announcement might have added, had lost its greatest statesman as well.

Local workers trudge home after a day's work at the Anglo-Persian oil refinery in Abadan. With rocketing demand for oil to power industry and transport, the Middle Eastern oil fields became a bone of international contention after the world war, even though their ouput at the time was small in comparison with that of the United States and the Soviet Union. In 1945, the area still produced only seven percent of the world supply.

JAPAN'S NEW HORIZONS

On a misty afternoon in May 1905, two powerful fleets of warships approached each other near the island of Tsushima in the strait between Japan and Korea. "The empire's fate depends on the result of this battle. Let every man do his utmost duty," the Japanese commander, Admiral Tōgō, signaled to the vessels sailing closely behind his flagship, the *Mikasa*.

Three miles across the water, the sailors and officers of the Russian Baltic fleet had just finished celebrating the anniversary of their czar's coronation. Having endured an arduous, dispiriting seven-month voyage halfway around the world, they were now eager to prove their worth against the navy of this upstart island nation, which for a decade had been disputing their claims to nearby Manchuria. As they took to their stations, however, they were astonished to find the Japanese line of battleships and cruisers executing a perfect 180-degree turn, a difficult and totally unexpected procedure that brought them on a parallel course to the Russian fleet. For a full ten minutes the Japanese presented a sitting target as they swung through the axis of the turn. But the Russians were unable to take advantage of the opportunity: While lining up into battle formation, they had become hopelessly muddled. "Mob is the only word literally to express our formation at this time," one officer later wrote. The poorly trained Russian gunners had hardly found their range before the Japanese completed their risky maneuver. Suddenly twelve modern warships released a merciless broadside on the disorganized Russian fleet. Observing the enemy through binoculars from the deck of the battleship *Suvorov*, Captain Simeonov could detect no signs of confusion:

> And what about us? I glanced around. Devastation! Flames on the bridges, burning debris on the deck, piles of bodies. Signaling, range-finding, and shot-spotting stations swept away and destroyed.

Whatever confidence the Russians may have initially felt soon evaporated as it became apparent that they could match the Japanese neither in speed nor in firepower. Their morale took a further blow at 3:30 p.m. when their flagship, *Oslyaba*, was sunk by enemy gunfire. Throughout the afternoon, the swift and disciplined Japanese fleet harried the crippled Russian squadron across the sea. The *Suvorov*, the *Kamchatka*, the *Borodino*, and the *Rousse* were all put out of action, and as the sun dropped below the horizon, the *Alexander III* exploded, leaving only, according to one observer, "a dense cloud of smoke that brooded over the place it had occupied."

As night finally fell over the debris-strewn waves off Tsushima, the sun was also setting over Russia's imperial ambitions in the Far East. The Japanese victory served as a potent symbol of a new political order. Just half a century before, Japan had been

Patriotic flags and paper lanterns bedeck a busy Yokohama street in May 1905 to celebrate Japan's naval victory over Russia at the Battle of Tsushima. Tsushima not only marked the climax of the fifteen-month Russo-Japanese War but also vindicated a program of modernization that, in the previous fifty years, had transformed Japan from a feudal backwater into a major world power. Material privations, such as high taxes, which the Japanese suffered to pay for this industrial and military growth, did little to dampen the wave of nationalistic fervor it engendered. The dual themes of national pride and territorial expansionism were to mark Japan's progress through the twentieth century.

an insular country, metaphorically as well as literally: Contacts with the rest of the world were strictly limited. Forced out of its isolation by Western nations eager to exploit its trading potential, Japan had embarked upon a course of revolutionary change. National pride and fear of the West had spurred the Japanese to transform their stratified feudal society into a modern industrialized state. By the turn of the century, the swords of samurai warriors filled the windows of curio shops, and modern factories produced the international currency of an industrial society—railways, steamships, communications technology, and armaments. Japan's triumph over Russia, climaxed by its crushing victory at Tsushima, revealed to the admiring, apprehensive Western world the extraordinary success of this policy.

Yet underlying the determined transition from ancient to modern was a political structure that contained the seeds of its own destruction. Holding the meteoric new state together was a precarious constitutional monarchy, the likes of which existed nowhere else in the world. Under the nominal rule of an emperor worshiped almost as a divinity, conflicting interests jostled for power. Elected politicians, giant business conglomerates, highborn elder statesmen, as well as an ambitious, impatient military establishment continually tested the limits of their influence in a domestic struggle that was to have a profound effect on the stability of the world. The eventual ascendancy of the military, more than twenty-five years after Tsushima, was to destroy the

Japan entered the twentieth century gripped by fervent nationalism. After more than fifty years of rapid modernization, it now had one of the most powerful armies in the world. The territorial expansion that its military leaders sought was not long in coming. In 1905, following war with Russia, Japan gained Port Arthur on Manchuria's Liaodong Peninsula, as well as half the northern island of Sakhalin; Korea was annexed just five years later; and after the Great War, Japan gained all of Germany's Pacific colonies above the equator, in addition to territory on the mainland Shandong Peninsula. An army sent into Siberia following the Russian Revolution of 1917 was eventually withdrawn in 1922. But further mainland expansion in Manchuria was less than a decade away.

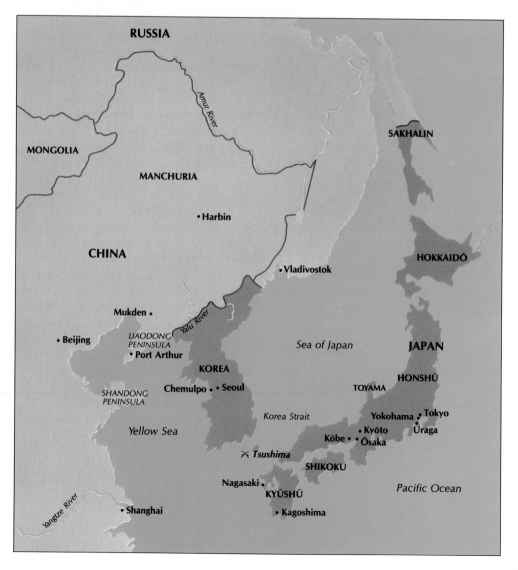

fragile edifice of Japanese politics and plunge half the earth into war.

To Western observers in the middle of the nineteenth century, Japan seemed a country that had fallen asleep. Since the 1630s, it had closed its doors to most European merchants and all European missionaries. Limited contacts with China and Korea satisfied most of the nation's material needs and kept it abreast of regional developments. Of the revolutions in politics, science, and industry that were transforming the Western world, however, all but a tiny elite remained in ignorance for 200 years. Any information a Japanese official or scholar succeeded in gleaning about Europe or the United States trickled through the southern port of Nagasaki, where a small colony of Dutch merchants were living in virtual isolation.

Depicted in 1854 as a mythical *tengu,* or goblin, U.S. commodore Matthew Perry scowls cross-eyed from a Japanese watercolor. Entrusted with the task of opening Japan to American diplomats and traders, Commodore Perry arrived with a show of force at the Japanese capital of Edo (later to become Tokyo) on July 8, 1853. The steamships in which he appeared terrified the Japanese, who thought that the barbarian intruders had "harnessed volcanoes." But when Perry returned the following year to complete his mission, he brought gifts that delighted the Japanese—among them a model steam train with its own track. One official insisted on riding the tiny locomotive, "whirling around a circular road . . . with his loose robes flying in the wind." Japan's romance with Western technology had begun.

The Japanese regarded their self-imposed seclusion as a blessing. The Great Peace, they called these years, and indeed, Japan enjoyed a domestic calm that would have been the envy of any nation. Underlying this tranquillity was a system of rigid feudal obligations. The country was divided into approximately 300 fiefs, each ruled by a lord, or daimyo, whose wealth came from a land tax imposed on his peasant subjects. Within his fief a daimyo kept order with a private army drawn from the samurai warrior caste, and he had a free hand to dispense justice and run the economy; but he owed ultimate allegiance to the nation's military governor, the shogun. Since 1603, these rulers had always been members of the Tokugawa family, Japan's most powerful warrior house. To guard against possible rebellion, the vassal daimyo was obliged to regularly attend the shogun's court in the eastern city of Edo, where members of his family remained all year as hostages to ensure his loyalty.

Curiously eclipsed by the shogun's court at Edo was another court—that of the emperor. The Japanese royal family, who traced its ancestry back to the sun goddess and the creation of the world, lived in isolated splendor in the central city of Kyōto. In theory the emperor ruled Japan with the assistance of the shogun as his military deputy; but in fact the servant had long since assumed the master's role. Sacrosanct but powerless, the court at Kyōto remained little more than a living museum until events of the mid-nineteenth century propelled it into the forefront of national affairs.

Japan's feudal society might well have survived into the twentieth century had not Westerners found its isolation irritating and its untapped potential for trade irresistible. Piqued that these unknown islands, which lay tantalizingly near newly established trade routes to China, should refuse so much as to supply their ships or shelter their sailors, European and American merchants began to clamor for the "opening" of Japan. When conventional overtures failed to elicit a positive response from the shogunate, the United States sent four armed ships and a company of marines under

Commodore Matthew Perry "to bring a singular and isolated people into the family of civilized nations," as the commodore himself put it. The Japanese, completely unprepared to defend themselves against Western armaments, broke centuries of precedent and formally received the visitors. Landing at Uraga near the shogun's capital in July 1853, Perry delivered a friendly but insistent letter from U.S. President Millard Fillmore to the anxious Japanese officials who received him, and he promised to come back in the spring "with a much larger force."

When Perry returned the following February, the Japanese agreed to grant the United States consular status and to open up two ports where American ships could purchase supplies. Five years later, bowing to relentless pressure from Europe and America, Japan finally permitted Western merchants to trade in a few designated ports, granting the Western states jurisdiction over their own citizens on Japanese soil. It was the beginning of the end; within twenty years, two centuries of determined isolation would be completely undone.

One of the first casualties of the Western incursion was the shogun. His inability to resist Western demands had undermined his authority in the eyes of many Japanese. Therefore, several wealthy and independent-minded daimyo began to condemn the Edo court as corrupt and inefficient. Seeking a figurehead for their discontent, they rediscovered the court at Kyōto and found in the emperor an invaluable source of spiritual leadership. Revere the Emperor; Expel the Barbarians became the rallying cry of the shogun's disaffected vassals and their samurai retainers.

But during a decade of sporadic violence and increasing instability, it grew clear that the "barbarians" were there to stay. After 1864, when British warships reduced the fiercely nationalistic town of Kagoshima to ashes in retaliation for the murder of an English citizen, any serious thoughts of driving foreigners from Japan began to fade. Those who argued that learning from the newcomers was the only way to preserve Japan's independence now held sway.

The end of the shogunate was accomplished with surprisingly little bloodshed. Under the banner of the emperor, antishogun forces steadily grew in strength. In January 1868, a group of rebels, notably warriors from the southwestern domains of Choshu and Satsuma, announced that all power had been transferred to the fifteen-year-old emperor, Meiji. By the spring of that year, unable to resist the rebel forces, the shogun had surrendered and his supporters had fled. Having engineered the rebirth of imperial rule—an event later known as the Meiji Restoration—Japan's new strongmen set about replacing the discredited feudal government.

From the beginning, the leaders of the Meiji state stressed the importance of military strength combined with political, economic, and social reforms based on Western models. Enrich the Country; Strengthen the Army was the new cry. Whatever they decided, moreover, would be seen to originate not from them but from the emperor. Accordingly, in April 1868, the young Meiji issued his Charter Oath, whose five articles defined the philosophy of the new regime. The last article encapsulated the unique marriage of East and West that was to typify Japan's development throughout the century: "Knowledge shall be sought all over the world so as to strengthen the foundations of imperial rule."

The new leaders—or imperial advisers, as they saw themselves—wasted no time in adapting Western institutions to domestic needs. In the years since Commodore Perry's appearance, the Japanese had learned much about life outside the islands, both from Western visitors and from sending out their own fact-finding delegations.

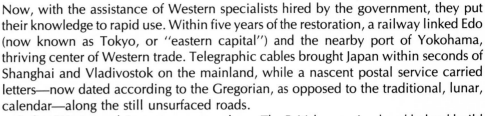

Now, with the assistance of Western specialists hired by the government, they put their knowledge to rapid use. Within five years of the restoration, a railway linked Edo (now known as Tokyo, or "eastern capital") and the nearby port of Yokohama, thriving center of Western trade. Telegraphic cables brought Japan within seconds of Shanghai and Vladivostok on the mainland, while a nascent postal service carried letters—now dated according to the Gregorian, as opposed to the traditional, lunar, calendar—along the still unsurfaced roads.

At first Western advisers were everywhere. The British organized and helped build the Japanese navy. Americans shaped the banking and education systems. The police officers who patrolled the streets of Tokyo were tutored by the French, and the army and medical services were modeled along German lines.

The Meiji leaders' aim, however, was for Japan to learn the Western lessons so thoroughly that the European and American advisers would become unnecessary. "The Japanese only look upon foreigners as schoolmasters," complained one European. "As long as they cannot help themselves they make use of them; and then they send them about their business."

Japan was to be very successful in shaking off its dependence on the industrial West. Within ten years of the Meiji Restoration, two homemade steamships had

The twenty-five-year-old Meiji emperor sports European uniform for a formal portrait. A year after ascending the throne in 1867, at the age of fifteen, he adopted the reign name Meiji, or "enlightened rule." During his forty-four-year reign, Japan underwent a thorough program of Westernization. Though only a figurehead for policies devised by his statesmen, the emperor often led the way in adopting European customs. He began in 1872 by cutting his traditional topknot and wearing Western clothes. Whereas previous emperors had led secluded lives, this monarch rode around Tokyo in an open carriage and toured remote parts of the country as a visible symbol of the new order sweeping Japan.

sailed from the Nagasaki shipyards. And in 1892, the Japanese produced their first locomotive. Other industries central to a modern state—mining, communications, and armaments, for instance—were nursed through their unproductive infancies by the government until sufficient private capital became available.

Equally important changes were occurring on a smaller scale on the farms and in family businesses. New varieties of seeds and fertilizers greatly increased the output of Japan's peasant farmers, who constituted some 80 percent of the population of 40 million. Power machinery for spinning and weaving revolutionized the manufacture of textiles, transforming a traditional cottage industry into one of the early Meiji success stories.

New codes and decrees replaced centuries of political tradition. Among the early decisions of the Meiji leaders was the abolition of the feudal system, which, with its rigid class structure and inefficient fragmentation of the land into privately controlled fiefs, was a major stumbling block to change. The dissolution of the fiefs had begun in 1871; farmers were given private ownership of the land and released from all feudal controls; and the daimyo were removed from their administrative roles and given titles in a new, European-style peerage. More important perhaps, the private armies of the daimyo were disbanded, and a single new army of conscripts was raised to serve the nation.

This was indeed a social revolution. Although previously only the warrior caste of samurai had been permitted to carry weapons, now the son of any farmer or

A TASTE FOR WESTERN WAYS

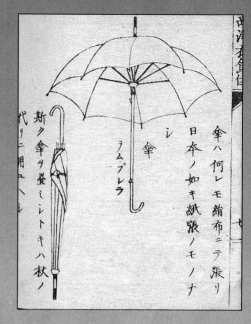

Originally apprehensive of the West, Japan's leaders soon realized that if they were ever to meet Europeans and Americans on equal terms, there was no alternative but to study and imitate them. Consequently, in December 1871, an embassy left the port of Yokohama for a tour of the United States and Europe. It was just the first of many such missions that reported back to the Japanese the road that the new state should take.

On the surface, the result was an outright aping of European customs, from art and literature down to the smallest details of personal hygiene. Europeans were both amused and irritated by the ill-fitting attire of the *haikara*—euphonically named after their high collars—who dressed in the latest Western fashions.

But Japan's government did not copy the West blindly: It chose carefully, combining political, military, and industrial institutions that best suited the nation. Its navy, for example, was modeled on that of Britain, its constitution on that of Germany. When, by the end of the 1800s, the vogue for Western habits subsided, Japan was left strengthened by the innovations and with its sense of identity intact.

Two years after the foundation of the Tokyo Music School, the class of 1889 wears European finery to perform a concert of Western music. The pianist is believed to be a noble who studied music at America's Vassar College.

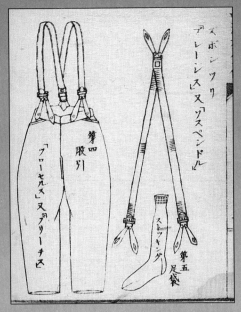

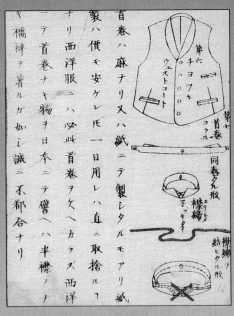

Umbrellas, suspenders, and collars are illustrated and analyzed in a detailed Japanese guide to Western customs. Published in 1867, the book was aimed at status-conscious Japanese, teaching them how to eat, dress, and even urinate in the Western style. Each drawing was labeled with ideograms and a phonetic rendering of the English pronunciation.

merchant was granted the privilege of dying in battle for the emperor. A further indignity lay in store for the old warriors when a new decree prohibited the wearing of swords, "the living soul of the samurai," whose razor-sharp blades could cut through a pile of copper coins without a nick.

Compulsory primary education also served as a leveler, giving the bright country boy a chance to compete with his more privileged contemporaries. In 1872, the Meiji leaders called for the establishment of about 54,000 primary schools—one for every 600 inhabitants—in the recognition that only an educated populace could maintain the new industrial state. Accordingly, schools taught the full range of practical subjects necessary for Japan to compete with the Western world.

This trend toward equality in education and military service, however, was to prove not so much a step toward democracy as a way of extending the traditional values of the samurai class to all the emperor's subjects. The aim of Yamagata Aritomo, one of the founders of the Meiji state and the father of Japan's modern army, was from the start to create a "citizen samurai"—obedient, fearless, and unswervingly devoted to the emperor.

The pace of Westernization had a dizzying effect on fashions and social customs in the cities. "To have lived through the transition stage of modern Japan," wrote one weary English professor at the newly established Tokyo University, "makes a man feel preternaturally old." Everything Western had its season: ballroom dancing, mesmerism and séances, athletics, cockfighting—there was even a brief craze for rabbit collecting. Government officials wore formal Western dress, complete with top hat, to work. Baseball came to stay, while tooth blackening and mixed bathing, traditions that Westerners found offensive, were discouraged.

Inevitably a reaction to Westernization set in, but it did not lead the Japanese to

A propaganda painting from the Sino-Japanese War of 1894-1895 portrays disciplined Japanese troops storming to victory at the Battle of Hai Chen. Following the arrival of Commodore Perry, Japan's rulers used the full arsenal of Western technology to build a modern army, replacing sailing ships and swords with steam-powered warships and guns. In 1873, compulsory military service was introduced for every able-bodied man. Despite initial resistance—20,000 peasants were arrested in anticonscription riots—the army had a reserve of 200,000 men by the 1890s. China's army, represented here as poorly armed and primitive, was in fact well equipped and powerful. Its collapse in 1895 surprised the world and revealed the strength of Japan's troops.

abandon modern technology: Factories continued to make cotton yarn and field guns. Nevertheless, the veneer of Western culture gradually lost its appeal, and by the 1880s, many of the Japanese elite were rediscovering the values they had discarded so hastily in 1868. A foreigner in Tokyo might notice only superficial changes, such as the gradual reappearance of the kimono. But on a deeper level, the rediscovery of native traditions reflected a renewed sense of national identity that soon shattered any Western dreams of Japan's becoming a Far Eastern extension of Europe.

Nowhere was this more evident than in the schoolroom. "A typical Japanese student," wrote one gratified European teacher at the end of the nineteenth century, "belongs to that class of youth who are the schoolmaster's greatest delight—quiet, intelligent, deferential, studious almost to excess." As such, these obedient youngsters were ideal material for indoctrination by an increasingly conservative government, which regarded education as a tool of the state. Japanese ethics and Chinese classics, deportment, and military drill ousted the liberal curriculum favored by early reformers. The cult of the emperor was emphasized in the classroom, where teachers and students alike were obliged to bow to his portrait every day. An imperial rescript, issued in 1890 to all schools, scarcely mentioned education, stressing instead the importance of obedient and "harmonious" conduct. "Should emergency arise," it urged, "offer yourself courageously to the State; and thus guard and maintain the prosperity of Our Imperial Throne coeval with heaven and earth."

Nationalism in the classroom was reinforced by the state's encouragement of the Shinto religion. Shinto, meaning "way of the gods," was a relatively unstructured fusion of ancestor and nature worship, recognizing 800 or more deities—including wind, ocean, trees, pestilence, and fire—to whom priests offered prayers and presented ritual offerings of food in simple thatched temples. As a homegrown Japanese belief celebrating the divine origins of the imperial family, Shinto was particularly attractive to the Meiji leaders. Not only Japan, but also an unbroken line of Japanese emperors, it was believed, traced their origins to the mythological Shinto deities Izanagi and Izanami. An additional attraction of Shinto to Japanese nationalists was that—unlike Christianity or Buddhism—it offered no moral precepts or spiritual theory that might undermine the centrality of the emperor.

The group of men presiding over these policies, former court officials and middle-ranking members of the samurai class, shared responsibility with a selflessness that would have been hard to achieve in a Western country undergoing a similar transformation. Although there were natural leaders among the so-called Meiji oligarchs, no one man attempted to seize dictatorial powers. Serious disagreements, when they did occur, ended not with long knives but with dignified resignations.

The Meiji oligarchs were not cynically using the emperor's name in order to gain support for state policy; they consulted him on important issues and seriously considered his advice. "His Majesty's decisions inclined almost invariably toward liberal and progressive ideas," wrote Itō Hirobumi, an admirer of the emperor and one of the most respected Meiji leaders. But the oligarchs in no way felt bound by the emperor's wishes. In so doing they were following time-honored precedent: For much of the nation's history, neither shoguns nor emperors had exercised total power over state policy; a council of advisers—influential though often nameless—had long been the true governing force behind Japan's nominal rulers.

From the beginning of their rule, it was the aim of the Meiji oligarchs to win for Japan, in the words of Itō Hirobumi, "the status of a civilized nation." To gain

acceptance from the democratic West, there had to be a significant indication that Japan was moving toward a more representative government. But the nation had no tradition of popular participation in politics and little concept of inalienable human rights. Furthermore, the Meiji leaders had reached manhood as samurai in Japan's old hierarchical society; there was small likelihood of their learning to march, in middle age, to the tune of Western liberalism.

The solution was a written constitution, largely the work of Itō himself, which took one resolute step into the future and another one back into the past. The constitution—in force from 1889—provided for a parliament comprising two houses. The upper house consisted of hereditary nobles or recently appointed members of Japan's new nobility. Members of the lower house were elected, and although less than five percent of the male population was at first entitled to vote, the body had the reassuring characteristics of a Western-style assembly.

Japan's new parliament, however, exercised little real power. There was no provision in the constitution for party government. The emperor, described as "sacred and inviolable," appointed ministers of state. More portentous still, the army and navy were answerable directly to no one except the emperor. In practice this meant that many of the leaders who had steered Japan through its early years continued at the helm, duly taking turns as ministers in the newly formed cabinet. During his long life in government, Itō was prime minister on four occasions. Even when party politicians finally began to assume power, forty years or so after the restoration, the remaining elder statesmen—or genro, as they became known—exercised an enormous influence over Japan's domestic and foreign policy.

Although they took limited steps to broaden Japan's political system, the Meiji leaders never lost sight of the second half of their rallying cry: Strengthen the Army. Since the restoration, Japan's army and navy had grown dramatically in strength and efficiency. Every able-bodied man could expect to spend three years in uniform on national service and an additional nine years in the reserves. With a potential fighting force of 200,000, Japanese leaders began to take an active interest in foreign affairs.

They did not have far to look. Less than 150 miles to the west, stretching toward Japan like an uncompleted bridge from the Asian mainland, was the peninsula of Korea. A rickety, antiquated state, Korea was vulnerable to any predator. Even moderate Japanese could appreciate the threat that Korea would pose to the nation's security if it fell into the hands of a hostile power. Belligerent parties favored immediate action to prevent any such occurrence.

The warmongers had their opportunity in 1894, when a rebellion in Korea brought Japan and China into direct confrontation. China had long considered Korea its own tributary state and the Korean king little more than a Chinese government minister—a situation the Japanese were unwilling to accept. Both countries sent troops to crush the rebellion, and once the job was done, neither side wanted to leave. When attempts to negotiate a troop withdrawal failed, Japan's military machine was unleashed. It struck with a speed and violence that took the world by surprise. China's army was no match for the disciplined and patriotic Japanese, whose officers were eager to prove themselves in battle. By February 1895, six months after the outbreak of hostilities, the Sino-Japanese War was over and Japan was the winner.

In the wake of this conflict, the Japanese nation was seized by patriotic fervor. Voices of moderation in parliament fell silent in the euphoria of victory. According to Foreign Minister Mutsu Munemitsu, the people were "only concerned about the date when the Japanese flag would be carried through the gates of Beijing."

In the ensuing Treaty of Shimonoseki, Japan stopped short of demanding Beijing but did exact from China a handsome war indemnity. Furthermore, China agreed to respect the independence of Korea and to cede the island of Formosa (today's Taiwan) to Japan. The greatest of Japan's gains, however, was the strategic Liaodong Peninsula, a southern extension of Manchuria projecting into the sea immediately northwest of Korea. At its tip was Port Arthur, a naval base that controlled access to the north China coast. The security of Japan seemed assured.

But the victory celebrations were short-lived. Just a week after the treaty was ratified, Russia, Germany, and France "advised" Japan to give up the Liaodong Peninsula. Two days later, Russia spelled out this advice in threatening detail. Japan's control of the Liaodong Peninsula would, according to Russia, be "a perpetual obstacle to peace in the Far East." Realizing that diplomatic language like this was just a step away from a declaration of war, Japan's leaders surrendered their claims to the disputed peninsula.

If the aim of the Triple Intervention, as it became known, was to teach Japan a lesson, it failed miserably. The Great Powers had not destroyed the wasp's nest that hung by their back door; they had merely plugged up the opening and given it a good shake. Japan, it is true, attempted no resistance to the Triple Intervention, but its

Intervention in China

A sharp boost to Japan's international standing came in 1900. In that year, local Chinese militia groups, known to Europeans as Boxers, rose against all foreigners intervening in their country's affairs. On June 10, tacitly supported by China's empress dowager, they murdered two diplomats—one of whom was Japanese—and laid siege to the British legation in Beijing, where the entire foreign community had taken refuge.

An international relief force of some 20,000, of which 8,000 Japanese troops formed by far the largest contingent, succeeded in raising the siege on August 14. When victorious officers of the Japanese, German, Russian, British, French, and American armies rode into Beijing's Forbidden City (left), it was a humiliating blow to China's pride. For Japan it was a welcome recognition of equality with the West.

people reacted with grief and anger, the effects of which were to reverberate well into the twentieth century.

Far from allaying fears about foreign aggression on the mainland, the effect of the Sino-Japanese War was to increase Japan's sense of insecurity. Swept by a tide of nationalism, the Japanese people stoically withstood soaring taxes in order to lavish more money on the armed forces. The budget for the army in 1896 was more than triple that of 1893, and over the next decade, the number of troops on active service nearly doubled. By 1906, Japan's navy, with seventy-six major warships, was thought to be one of the strongest and most modern in the world.

A galling coda to Japan's brush with the Great Powers occurred in 1898, when Russia seized the Liaodong Peninsula for itself, finding in Port Arthur the warm-water port it had long coveted.

It was not long before Japan had an opportunity to test its strengthened army in the field. In 1899, a nationalist Chinese group, the Society of the Fists of Righteous Harmony, rose to prominence in China. Its members, who became known as Boxers from their ritualistic practice of shadowboxing, which they believed conferred immunity from Western bullets, began to agitate for the expulsion of all aliens—the "foreign devils," as the Chinese called them. In that category, to their indignation, were included the Japanese. The movement reached a climax the following year when the Boxers besieged the foreign legations in Beijing. The 20,000-strong allied army that finally put down the Boxers included 8,000 Japanese troops. Throughout the campaign, Foreign Minister Aoki Shuzo had insisted on cooperating with the other powers; it would have been quite possible, however, for Japan alone to crush the rebellion at an earlier point. The efficiency of Japan's army and the diplomatic way in which Japan conducted itself earned the respect of the international community.

A more tangible reward came Japan's way two years later. Of the four European powers with interests in the Far East, only Britain had refrained from intervening after Japan's war with China. Furthermore, British technical advisers, chiefly to Japan's expanding navy, had helped promote friendly relations between the two countries. It still came as a remarkable recognition of Japan's newly en-

Wearing white armbands, natives of Port Arthur—possibly rescue workers—crouch against a desolate backdrop of foundered Russian warships sunk by Japanese artillery on December 7, 1904. The seemingly impregnable Russian outpost of Port Arthur, situated on the Manchurian peninsula of Liaodong, was a major strategic objective in the Russo-Japanese War. On February 8, 1904, two days before war was even declared, Japanese torpedo boats had attacked and severely damaged the Russian fleet stationed there. Port Arthur fell on January 2, 1905, after a six-month siege that cost the Japanese 20,000 casualties. The war ended just four months later, following Russia's defeat at Tsushima.

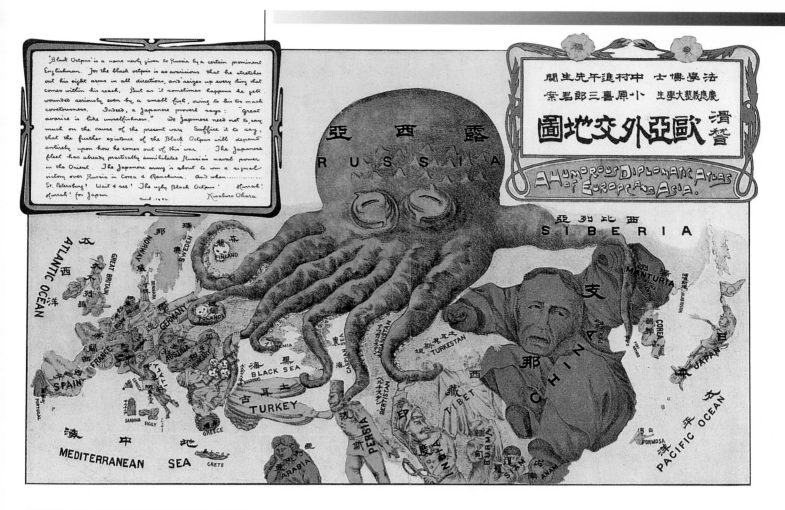

A Japanese propaganda handbill published in March 1904 portrays Russia as a predatory black octopus, strangling every nation within reach of its tentacles. Russia's aggressive policy in the Far East was viewed with alarm not only by Japan but also by Britain and the United States—for whose benefit the cartoon's English-language caption was provided. Other countries, however, were worried by Japan's growing strength. France feared that a war might weaken its ally, Russia, and Kaiser Wilhelm of Germany was apprehensive that a Russian defeat might set off a revolution that could spread to his own country. The kaiser in his turn commissioned a picture of his own personal design that showed Japan as a "yellow peril" threatening the West.

hanced status when Great Britain and Japan announced a formal alliance in 1902.

The Anglo-Japanese alliance guaranteed that if one of the partners went to war against a single power, the other would maintain a friendly neutrality. If two or more powers allied themselves against either Japan or Great Britain, however, the other would be obliged to join the conflict. As Britain saw it, this agreement would ensure the safety of British interests in the mainland Yangtze Valley. It would also serve as a warning to the Russians, who had been reinforcing their troops in Manchuria ever since the Boxer Rebellion, ostensibly to protect the newly built railway line between Port Arthur and Harbin, in the north. "We are allying ourselves to one of the pluckiest little nations in the world," said one condescending British member of Parliament.

To expansionist officers and politicians in Japan, on the other hand, the alliance amounted to an invitation to war with Russia. With the guarantee of British protection, they believed, neither France nor Germany would be tempted to enter the fray. After a decade of intense military preparation, Japan felt the equal of any single power. A victory over Russia would be a popular antidote to ten years of humiliation.

Imperial Russia was not at all alarmed by the prospect of war. Czar Nicholas II, who as crown prince had almost lost his life in an assassination attempt while visiting Japan in 1891, privately referred to Japanese diplomats as "monkeys." His contempt was shared by most of his closest advisers. "We will only have to throw our caps at them and they will run away," asserted one general. An easy victory in the Far East would not only establish Russian control over Manchuria; it would help ease domestic problems as well. "What this country needs is a short, victorious war to stem the tide of revolution," said the minister of the interior to the minister of war.

Leaders in Japan were divided over the wisdom of war with Russia. Prime Minister Katsura Tarō, a protégé of the venerable Yamagata Aritomo, urged action; Itō Hirobumi, Yamagata's old colleague and rival, argued for continued negotiations, and for a while he prevailed. Discussions over the Russian presence in Manchuria and Japanese intentions in Korea dragged on for months. In January 1904, infuriated by Russian procrastination, the Katsura government issued an ultimatum: Both countries were to respect the territorial integrity of Korea and China (of which Manchuria was still officially a part); Japan agreed that Russia had the right to protect its railway in Manchuria but insisted on its own military and economic privileges in Korea. Russia responded by reinforcing its troops in Manchuria along the Korean border.

The Japanese did not wait upon the nicety of declaring war before delivering their riposte. While the bulk of the Russian fleet was lying at anchor in Port Arthur, a squadron of Japanese destroyers launched a torpedo attack under cover of darkness. Several Russian ships were damaged and two battleships ran aground in the ensuing chaos, half-blocking the narrow mouth of the harbor. The effect of this sudden action, coupled with a timid and indecisive Russian naval command, was to give Japan the freedom of the seas for the duration of the war.

With the Russian navy neutralized, Japan encountered no opposition in landing troops at Chemulpo (present-day Inch'ŏn), port of the Korean capital of Seoul. Pushing the Russians north across the Yalu River, they advanced rapidly into Manchuria. Meanwhile, a second Japanese army landed on the Liaodong Peninsula and marched south to besiege the heavily defended city of Port Arthur.

In the battles that followed, the Russian army, though large and well equipped, proved itself no match for its superbly trained and fanatically courageous opponents. "It is impossible not to admire the bravery and activity of the Japanese," wrote General Kuropatkin, the Russian commander in chief, who had initially opposed the war. To his officers he issued the following discouraging description of the enemy in battle: "The attack of the Japanese is a continuous succession of waves, and they never relax their efforts by day or by night."

For five months the Russian soldiers at Port Arthur defended their positions with grim determination, at times hurling rocks upon the enemy from their hilltop fortifications when ammunition ran short. With no hope of reinforcements, however, the garrison stood little chance against the seemingly infinite number of Japanese, and the town surrendered on January 2, 1905. On the northern front, the campaign climaxed in a massive struggle for the key city of Mukden. Here, in deep snow and arctic cold, 400,000 Japanese overwhelmed a Russian army only slightly smaller in size. Japanese casualties, at 70,000, outnumbered the Russian losses by more than three to one, but it was this victory that finally crushed their opponents' will to resist.

All eyes were now on the Russian Baltic fleet, which had set sail in October 1904. It made a tragicomic sight. Convinced by an overenthusiastic spy that the North Sea was full of Japanese torpedo boats, the fleet was vigilant—so vigilant, in fact, that during the nighttime crossing one drunken captain fired 296 shots at various commercial ships under the impression that they were hostile vessels. By the time it reached the Atlantic, the Baltic fleet's bag included several British fishermen and the chaplain of the Russian cruiser *Aurora*, which had appeared in an unexpected place. To this score it added, in Tangier, the international telegraph cable linking Africa and Europe, which caught in an anchor and was cut to save delay. And off Madagascar, where the crew received news of Port Arthur's fall, along with a surprising shipment of 12,000 pairs of boots and vast quantities of fur-lined winter coats, Russian gunners performing their drill sent two shells into the bridge of one of their own cruisers and scored another hit on the unfortunate *Aurora* while saluting a burial. They arrived in the Far East the following May, after a headlong dash across the Indian Ocean.

Although it came too late to win the war, the Russians hoped that this powerful but outdated force might at least restore their military prestige and allow them to achieve a satisfactory negotiated settlement. The Baltic fleet's final debacle in the Strait of Tsushima had precisely the opposite effect. After two days of fighting, Russia had lost thirty-four ships and nearly 12,000 men, to Japan's three ships and 110 men. The Russians had nothing left with which to reply. When U.S. President Roosevelt offered to host peace talks, they gratefully accepted.

Under the Treaty of Portsmouth, which ended the war on September 5, 1905, Japan's unique relationship with the "independent" state of Korea was formally acknowledged. The Russians agreed to withdraw from Manchuria, leaving to Japan

Vendors sell fruit and bottled drinks to German prisoners of war at a depot in the Japanese port of Ōita. During the Great War, about 8,000 Germans, including 5,000 civilians, were interned by the Japanese, who entered the war as an ally of Britain's. Although Japan played only a small part in the fighting, it made important territorial gains, seizing the Chinese town of Jiaozhou and other mainland German bases, as well as most of Germany's island colonies in the Pacific. After the war, the victorious Allies agreed that Japan could retain German possessions north of the equator. Australia, however, fearful of the "yellow peril," refused to sanction Japanese expansion to the south.

Port Arthur, their railway, and other valuable interests in the Liaodong Peninsula. Japan also acquired half the northern island of Sakhalin and associated fishing rights. But for many Japanese, this was not enough. The announcement of the terms infuriated those anticipating a generous indemnity from Russia to compensate for the huge cost of the war. Nor did the agreement satisfy a newly influential military establishment, whose hunger for territory would increasingly motivate foreign policy.

Compared with the expenses and sacrifice of the Russo-Japanese War, the next fifteen years seemed almost a gift to Japan's expansionist military. After the noisy protests that followed the Treaty of Portsmouth, Japan's quiet annexation of Korea in 1910 was practically an anticlimax. Over the years, Japan had assumed all but complete control of its defenseless neighbor, appointing the grand old statesman Itō Hirobumi as resident general in control of Korea's foreign affairs. The assassination of Itō by a Korean nationalist provided a suitable pretext to justify the final move. Contingency plans were put into operation, and Korea—for all but the resentful Koreans—effectively ceased to exist.

The Great War of 1914-1918 provided a further opportunity for territorial gain. At the outbreak of hostilities, Britain requested Japanese help in defending its Chinese interests. Japan, seeing no gain from such a limited involvement, insisted on a full declaration of war against Germany, thereby gaining an opportunity to expand into China. With now familiar speed and efficiency, Japan invaded the Chinese mainland and captured German bases on the Shandong Peninsula, extending out into the Yellow Sea toward Korea. It also seized the Mariana, Caroline, and Marshall islands, German possessions in the Pacific that offered little resistance. Six months after the war had broken out, while France was becoming a muddy graveyard for the youth of Europe, Japan was consolidating the spoils of victory.

With the Great Powers preoccupied on the other side of the globe, the Japanese gave free rein to their desire for control of the Asian mainland. In 1915, they presented China with a list of conditions asserting Japan's dominant role in continental politics. The so-called Twenty-One Demands insisted on a transfer of former German property to Japan. More controversial, they called for Japanese advisers to "assist" Chinese authorities in the direction of China's military, economic, and political affairs. Though powerless to prevent the occupation of the Shandong Peninsula, China drew the line at agreeing to this demand. In so doing it almost certainly saved itself from becoming another Korea.

Another international incident near the end of the war revealed the expansionist mood in Japanese politics.

Bury the Corrupt Politicians is one of the slogans touted at a 1920s demonstration by a group of Japanese suffragettes, clad in the latest Western fashions. Women were essential to Japan's industrialization, comprising more than 80 percent of textile workers. For the most part, though, they were left behind by the wave of emancipation that swept the Western world in the first quarter of the twentieth century. Coming low in Japan's traditional hierarchy, women were invariably poorly paid and, after work, were confined to factory dormitories for ease of supervision. The right to attend public meetings had been won in 1922, but it was not until 1946 that they received the right to vote.

When disorders associated with the Bolshevik Revolution threatened to destabilize eastern Siberia, the Allies agreed to send a peacekeeping force to the area around Vladivostok. The Japanese army leaped at this opportunity for an advance into northern Asia. Despite efforts in parliament to limit the size of Japan's contingent, the nation's increasingly independent military establishment was in no mood to be checked. A total of some 70,000 men fanned out across Manchuria and Siberia, where they remained until well after the emergency had ended.

"Our empire is in the process of effecting a great change in the present world's situation," announced Prime Minister Ōkuma Shigenobu at the beginning of the war. "Without a doubt our empire is advancing toward the attainment of a status of parity with the most civilized nations in the world." His optimism appeared to be well grounded when Japan—despite its modest contribution to the war effort—claimed a place of importance next to the victorious Allies at the Paris Peace Conference of 1919. Although the Western powers listened sympathetically to China's vigorous protests, they agreed that Japan should keep the territory it had seized from Germany

Japanese workers gather proudly in an engine shed in the peninsula of Chita. Initially dependent on Western imports, Japan rapidly built up a strong industrial base. By the time this photograph was taken in 1919, the nation had achieved its twin aims of modernization and economic self-sufficiency. A ready supply of cheap labor existed to work in the busy factories; and by colonizing mainland countries such as Korea, Japan gained a captive market for the manufactured goods, especially textiles, on which its economy depended.

in Shandong. The Pacific islands were left in Japanese hands with little discussion.

Despite these acquisitions, the treaty of 1919 caused much bitterness. Attempts by Japan to insert a clause recognizing racial equality in the covenant of the League of Nations were thwarted by Western leaders—notably those of Australia and America—who wanted to maintain discriminatory immigration laws against a possible "yellow tide." For all their military and economic muscle, the Japanese had reason to believe that the "civilized nations" still regarded them as fundamentally inferior.

By this time, Japan certainly looked like a modern industrial nation. "The largest cities have completely changed their appearance by the construction of straight thoroughfares," commented one guidebook for Western travelers. "Excellent motor roads now connect the cities of Yokohama and Kobe and Ōsaka." Moreover, thanks to the ever-larger and more-powerful steamships that plied the oceans, a tourist in Yokohama was now only about ten days from North America and forty days from Europe. As for Tokyo, "Everywhere overhead is a network of telegraph, telephone, and electric wires," although the cherry trees in April could still "transform the town into a garden of blossoms." Not all Japanese appreciated these changes. "Tokyo appears to me nothing but a branch shop of London," complained one influential radical, expressing an anti-Western attitude that was growing in strength among certain nationalist organizations.

The population was growing, too—from 44 million in 1901 to 55 million soon after the war. The problems of housing and feeding these additional mouths fueled the arguments of those who advocated territorial expansion. To many Japanese, the empty spaces of Manchuria seemed the most logical home for these new citizens. As the venerable genro Yamagata put it, "Manchuria is Japan's lifeline."

But who was going to catch the rope? The Meiji emperor had died in 1912, to be succeeded by his son Yoshihito, known as the Taisho emperor. The influence of the original Meiji genro had finally begun to slacken.

Working-class flood victims of Tokyo's Tsukishima district jostle to buy cheap rice offered as a relief measure in 1917. Tsukishima was typical of the many developments that grew up around Japan's major cities to cater to the country's expanding population. In the 1870s, peasants began flocking from the overcrowded countryside to search for work, food, and shelter in Japan's new industrial centers. Those who had the necessary skills found jobs in the munitions factories that supplied the burgeoning army or as construction workers on the many building projects. At the start of the Meiji era, 80 percent of Japan's people were peasants; by 1921, only 50 percent of the population worked on the land.

In 1909, recent settlers on the island of Hokkaidō complete a temporary home built on newly cleared land, as part of a government project to increase Japan's arable area. With only 15 percent of the nation's mountainous landscape suitable for cultivation, farms were intensively worked and life was arduous. The modernization benefiting the rest of Japan did not extend to the countryside, where plots were generally too small and inaccessible for mechanized farming. Most families, unable to survive by farming alone, sent daughters and younger sons to work in the cities—with an unforeseen result. The tuberculosis that their children often contracted in unsanitary urban conditions was spread on visits home and became the major cause of death in rural Japan.

However, no political institution had emerged that could convincingly take the genro's place and lead a fully industrialized Japan into the twentieth century.

There were some progressives who placed their hopes in the growth of political parties. These had started to emerge even before the Constitution of 1889, but their development was continually stifled from above. The genro, true to their proud samurai origins, had little sympathy with popular political movements. When elected party members in the lower house began to obstruct the smooth functioning of the genro's rule, their leaders were bribed with cabinet posts and invited behind the closed doors of government committee rooms. So entrenched was their deference to authority that many politicians lost sight of their democratic principles in the awesome presence of the emperor's unelected advisers. Within the political parties themselves the situation was no more hopeful. One despairing liberal politician, writing in 1918, described the relationship between a party leader and his members as "similar to those that existed between a feudal lord and his liegemen."

Compromise and cooperation were the rules of Japan's political game. Corruption became another. A succession of bribery scandals emerged during the early decades of the century. To the cynical public, these were just fleeting glimpses of the extent to which business habitually influenced their government. The huge zaibatsu— family-run conglomerates such as Mitsubishi and Mitsui—had friends and relatives at every level of the administration. By 1930, more than 25 percent of the upper house and 12 percent of the members of the lower house had a commercial relationship with one of the zaibatsu concerns.

Many Japanese looked askance at the zaibatsu, seeing not a manifestation of a growing economy but instead a symbol of oppression. Although the war had brought an industrial boom, the benefits had passed mainly to the few—the *narikin,* or "new rich," as such war profiteers were called. Japanese leaders in industry and politics alike had shown little sympathy for the working conditions of the men and women who riveted the battleships or stitched the soldiers' uniforms. Not until 1916 was the maximum working day for women and children in cotton mills reduced, officially, to twelve hours. And in the countryside, the pressure of population on the limited area of cultivable land kept the rents paid by tenant farmers high. Many farmers, unable to support their families, sent their children to work in the textile mills; others kept body and soul together by selling their daughters as prostitutes to the detested narikin. But the greatest source of popular resentment was over the price of rice, which had risen steadily during the war years, fueled by the forward buying of speculators.

In the feudal days, such a rise would have been a boon to Japan's predominantly agricultural economy. But for an increasingly large, urban working class, it was unbearable. The storm burst in the summer of 1918, after the price of the staple had doubled in less than a year. That August, fishermen's wives in the western prefecture of Toyama rioted and forced a 10 percent price cut. It was a spark that ignited the whole country: In more than 350 cities, towns, and villages, rioting workers engaged in a wave of looting and arson. It took some 100,000 troops three weeks to quell the unrest, during which more than 100 people were killed and thousands arrested.

The response to the riots was a severe authoritarian backlash. Protest of any kind was dealt with sternly. Strikes were quickly suppressed and political parties that smacked of socialism instantly banned. Censorship of the press was rigidly enforced. So routinely were the newspapers prosecuted that they appointed "prison editors" to serve prison sentences while the real editor anonymously produced the paper.

The severest blow to individual liberty was the Peace Preservation Law, passed in 1925. Prompted by fears of Marxist subversion and a growing labor movement, it gave the police wide-ranging powers to deal with those who cherished "dangerous thoughts." It became, for example, a crime punishable by up to ten years in prison to join a society advocating any alteration of the national polity. Ironically, this measure came into force a week before enactment of the Universal Manhood Suffrage Act, which extended to every male of twenty-five years or older the right to vote.

These pieces of legislation were just two contrasting strands in the fabric of 1920s Japan. In outward appearance at least, the nation maintained a semblance of Western-style parliamentary government, with party cabinets made up of elected representatives. Japanese foreign policy, too, did much to heighten the impression of Western liberalism. "This administration attaches great importance to the League of Nations," said Baron Shidehara Kijuro, foreign minister for much of the decade. He also urged "the deepening of neighborly friendship" between Japan and China.

Shidehara's policies were as liberal as his words. He negotiated with the United States and Britain about naval limitation, agreeing in 1922 to a ratio of three Japanese capital ships to five each for the other powers. In the same year, responding to pressure from the United States, he presided over the withdrawal of Japanese troops from the Shandong Peninsula and the end of the military venture in Siberia.

At the same time, the younger generation of Japanese city dwellers were throwing themselves wholeheartedly into the Western way of life. Nowhere was this more obvious than in the universities—Tokyo had one of the largest student populations in the world—where wealthy, left-wing "Marx boys" were shocking their aristocratic parents with radical new ideas. And in sophisticated circles, the *Moga* and *Mobo* (contractions of the English "modern girl" and "modern boy") could be seen clad in

A few high-rise buildings, cherished symbols of progress, still stand amid the debris of central Tokyo following a devastating earthquake on September 1, 1923. More than half the capital, almost all of neighboring Yokohama, and many surrounding towns and villages were flattened. Then dry, warm weather combined with a strong wind to fuel fires that raged for three days. Some 100,000 people died, while millions more faced starvation, drought, and homelessness. Martial law was imposed to control the initial panic, and substantial aid from the United States—which had experienced a similar disaster in San Francisco seventeen years earlier—helped in the process of reconstruction. By 1927, the Imperial Palace was virtually all that remained of the ancient city of Edo.

the latest and flashiest fashions: cloche hats, short skirts, and bob haircuts for the Moga, voluminous Oxford bags for the Mobo.

Beneath the smooth surface of the so-called Liberal Twenties, however, a deep and irresistible current of angry frustration was gaining force. Ultranationalism was nothing new at the time, but it now began to extend from the extremist fringes of society, taking root as a widespread political conviction.

For years there had been nationalist societies, covert organizations that specialized in spying, international subversion, and political assassinations. The Amur Society, named after a Manchurian river, threatened liberal politicians and formed links with Chinese bandits in an attempt to destabilize Manchuria. For these organizations, businessmen and politicians were the cause of social evil. ''There is a great slackening of discipline and order,'' fulminated the Amur Society. ''The people are over-

whelmed by heavy taxes, the confusion of the business world complicates the livelihood of people, the growth of dangerous thought threatens social order." The ideals were harmony, simplicity, and obedience, qualities that the radicals believed were inherent in Japan's armed forces. Military discipline within the country and a policy of territorial expansion were the Amur Society's answers to most social problems.

Ultranationalism was given a boost by the United States in 1924. Spurred by fears of a supposed "yellow peril" in the western and southern states, Congress passed the National Origins Act, effectively barring additional Japanese immigration. Japanese nationalists, already convinced that America was seeking naval domination of the Pacific Ocean, saw this move as another call to arms.

By now, extreme forms of nationalism had permeated the army. Junior officers made little attempt to conceal their conviction that independent military action alone would purify the country; their superiors either turned a deaf ear to them or else listened sympathetically. "National reform" was their aim, and loyalty to the emperor their religion. (There were some, however, who wished that the scholarly young Hirohito, who succeeded the Taisho emperor in 1926, would show more enthusiasm for the patriotic activities of the army and navy.)

Disaffected young officers were incensed by Shidehara's decision to withdraw from Shandong and Siberia, as well as by the American immigration restriction. But it was while the country was reeling under the impact of the 1929 Wall Street crash, which crippled economies around the world, that the final insult came: Under the London Naval Treaty of 1930, it was agreed that the ratio of Japanese to American and British capital ships should be extended to cover auxiliary ships, an arrangement that many officers felt endangered Japan's security. This treaty had been forced through by the liberal prime minister Hamaguchi Osachi in defiance of the naval general staff. It was the last such show of independence by any civilian politician. In November 1930, Hamaguchi was shot by a civilian nationalist at the Tokyo railway station. He courageously tried to continue in office, but his injuries forced him to resign, and he died the next August. A month later, as if released by Hamaguchi's death, the army finally took the independent action it had long contemplated.

Matters started innocuously enough. On September 19, 1931, the Japanese learned from their morning papers that "a group of lawless Chinese bandits" had tried to blow up the Japanese-controlled Harbin–Port Arthur railway near the Manchurian town of Mukden. It later became clear that Japanese officers had planned and executed the incident, but at the time, it gave the Japanese army an excuse to extend its control northward. Within five months, despite protests from civilian politicians, the League of Nations, and the emperor, the army had seized all Manchuria, which it now forced Tokyo to recognize as the independent state of Manchukuo.

For almost eighty years, Japan had struggled to gain parity with the West. Its success, however, had paradoxically served to strengthen its own sense of national purpose and identity. As the emperor stood aloof, parliamentary liberals struggled unavailingly against the forces of ultranationalism, spearheaded by the military. By 1931, Japan's armed forces were strong enough to pursue their own goals without fear of Western intervention, and in this sense, the Manchurian incident represented the culmination of Japan's process of rebirth. In another, it marked the triumph of the nation's military establishment over its civilian government. Above all, it set a disciplined and increasingly chauvinistic state on the road that was to lead it to eventual disaster in the Second World War.

DAWN OF THE AUTOMOBILE AGE

In the early years of the twentieth century, Western nations embraced an invention that was to revolutionize land transport: the automobile. By the end of the 1920s, the car not only would have brought mobility to millions but also would have changed the face of society.

The key to the car's success was internal combustion, a principle understood in its crudest expression since the firing of the first gun. Not until the late nineteenth century, however, was the confined force of an explosion—produced by the ignition of such substances as petroleum or benzene—widely harnessed as a means of locomotive power. By 1900, following the work of German pioneers Carl Benz and Gottlieb Daimler, engineers worldwide were producing gasoline-driven road vehicles, dubbed horseless carriages.

These early cars—affordable only to the wealthy—vibrated uncomfortably and were unreliable, noisy, and slow (the 1897 Benz, above, could manage only eighteen miles per hour). Nevertheless, they were more biddable than horses, and compared with steam engines and their attendant fire hazards, or with electric vehicles and their bulky, short-lived accumulators, they were paragons of mobility.

As the twentieth century progressed, cars became more sophisticated and more widely available. Mass-production techniques, perfected by the American manufacturer Henry Ford in 1913, set prices on a downward spiral that brought cars to an ever-wider market. And the use of motorized vehicles in the Great War boosted production still further, while accelerating technological advance: Superchargers, for example, developed by wartime aeroengineers to increase engine power, were later adopted by the auto industry.

At the same time, war familiarized people with the car, and many servicemen returned home in 1919 eager to acquire their own vehicles. Bereft of war work, factories hastily regeared to meet the demand, and in the affluent 1920s, automobile production soared around the world. The epicenter of this increase was in the United States. The 2.5 million cars on American roads in 1915 had become 27 million by 1929, by which time motorized transportation had substantially affected the way people lived. In answer to a comment that her family owned a car but no bathtub, one American housewife replied, "Why, you can't go to town in a bathtub!" The world had entered the Age of the Automobile.

Most early cars, including this 1903 De Dion Bouton, had no roof or windshield; passengers donned caps, goggles, face masks, and gloves to protect themselves from the elements and from the dust their cars stirred up. The car's small lamps ran on oil rather than on electric current. Since most roads did not have streetlights at the time, even this meager light source lessened the hazards of night travel.

A POLISHED PRODUCT

The early "horseless carriages" proved worrisome status symbols to their wealthy owners. The engine, mounted on a traditionally styled carriage, had to be coaxed into life by turning a hand crank or by pulling on a flywheel; primitive controls meant that changing gears was no mean feat; and solid rubber tires made travel a bone-jarring experience.

Automobile manufacturers, drawn from occupations as diverse as electrical engineering and bicycle making, were quick to work on the problems. Inflatable tires were one advancement, and by the 1920s, shock absorbers helped smooth the ride even more. Improved gear systems and the electric starter reduced the amount of brute force required for motoring.

Amid the technological progress, traditional coach-building skills were not forgotten. Many firms made only the mechanical components, and then referred buyers to craftsmen who would custom-build the body. Clients could request such costly extras as ostrich-hide upholstery and rosewood dashboards.

The bodywork of this English sedan, a 1928 Bean Short 14, shows that by the 1920s, automobiles were no longer simply playthings for fine-weather excursions but were now integrated into everyday life. This Bean had a top speed of fifty-five miles per hour; nevertheless, as the toolbox on the running board testifies, maintenance and adjustment were frequent chores.

THE CONVEYOR-BELT CAR

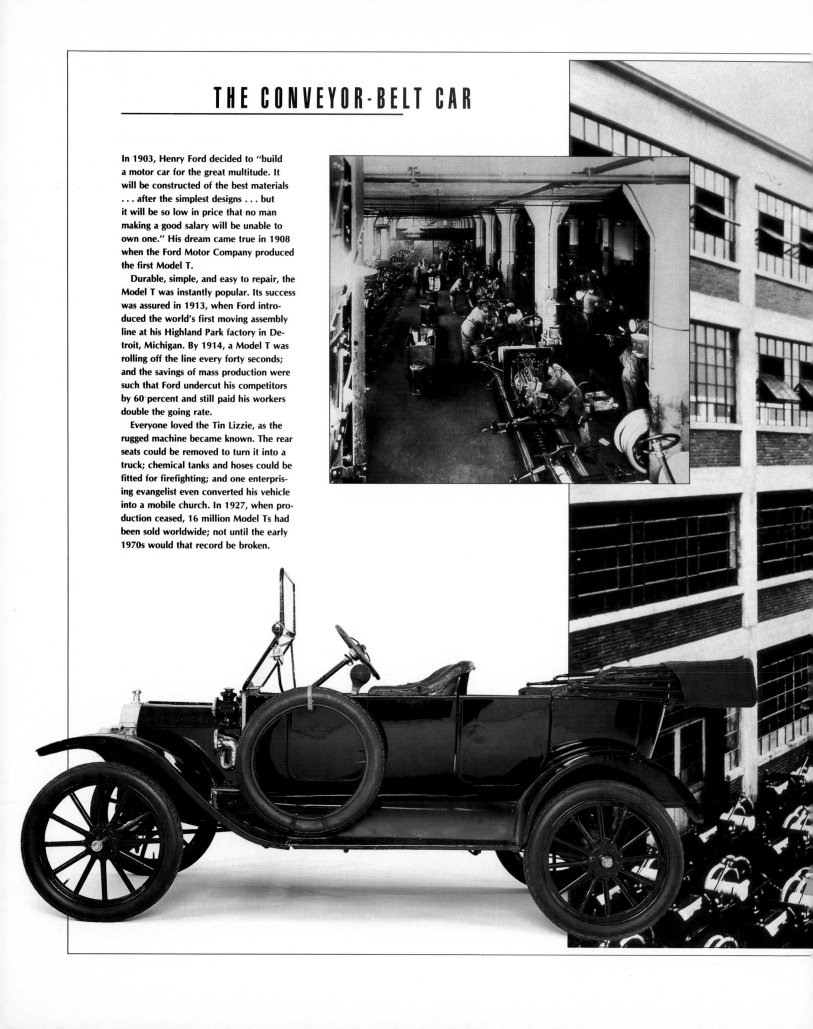

In 1903, Henry Ford decided to "build a motor car for the great multitude. It will be constructed of the best materials . . . after the simplest designs . . . but it will be so low in price that no man making a good salary will be unable to own one." His dream came true in 1908 when the Ford Motor Company produced the first Model T.

Durable, simple, and easy to repair, the Model T was instantly popular. Its success was assured in 1913, when Ford introduced the world's first moving assembly line at his Highland Park factory in Detroit, Michigan. By 1914, a Model T was rolling off the line every forty seconds; and the savings of mass production were such that Ford undercut his competitors by 60 percent and still paid his workers double the going rate.

Everyone loved the Tin Lizzie, as the rugged machine became known. The rear seats could be removed to turn it into a truck; chemical tanks and hoses could be fitted for firefighting; and one enterprising evangelist even converted his vehicle into a mobile church. In 1927, when production ceased, 16 million Model Ts had been sold worldwide; not until the early 1970s would that record be broken.

Uncompleted Model Ts are ranked outside the Highland Park factory *(below)*, ready for the final stage in production: the fitting of the body *(inset, right)*. To reach this stage, the car had already passed along an assembly line *(inset, left)*, where workers performed the repetitive task of fitting a designated number of the 2,000 parts that made up each vehicle.

SELLING THE DREAM

Initially, car manufacturers strove simply to present a generic concept of their products to the public. The Thousand-Mile Trial of 1900, for example, zigzagging from London to Edinburgh, was intended to show Britons—many tens of thousands of whom had never even seen a car—that the new machine was a viable alternative to the horse. By 1907, however, when a Turin-built Itala won a much-publicized 10,000-mile race from Beijing to Paris, people not only knew what a car looked like but were learning to distinguish between different models.

As the number of automobile manufacturers—many of them small firms catering to local needs—swelled, promotion shifted in emphasis. Each carmaker was now at pains to establish his automobile's own personality, and advertisements extolled the speed and power of a particular marque, or the lifestyle of opulence and leisure its owners enjoyed.

An image of classy leisure promotes this American Pierce Arrow in 1910.

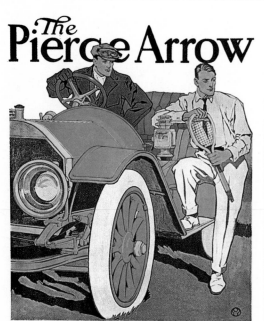

THE six-cylinder idea is no more a rightful adjunct of the Pierce-Arrow Car than are a hundred other sound ideas of car construction that we have adopted after a thorough trying out. Luxury means efficiency always.

THE PIERCE-ARROW MOTOR CAR COMPANY, BUFFALO, N.Y.

Comfortably in hand, a mid-range Italian Fiat presents no problems for its relaxed owner in 1923.

LE PETIT POUCET MONTAIT UNE PEUGEOT

Pierre Simmar

AUTOMOBILES
PEUGEOT

Seven-league boots are no
match for the speed of this
1907 French Peugeot as
it whisks its muster of
fairy-tale gnomes to safety.

Restrained but elegant, a
Daimler Mercedes fits the
trends of prewar Germany.

MERCEDES

DAIMLER
Motoren-Gesellschaft
Stuttgart-Unterfürkheim

Myth and manufacturing
muscle combine to pro-
mote the horsepower of a
1925 Italian Fiat.

FIAT 509

FREEDOM ON WHEELS

The independence conferred by car ownership set whole populations on the move. In the United States, the transcontinental Lincoln Highway and other new roads helped millions gain access to national parks. The American family shown here picnicking by their Model T was just one of many who used their newfound freedom to discover the joys of outdoor life.

Inevitably, the environment changed to reflect the new mobility. Suburbs burgeoned to accommodate car-owning city dwellers in search of cheaper rents and better living conditions; businesses, too, moved to city outskirts, where parking space was plentiful. Farther out, tourist homes and campgrounds sprang up to provide facilities for sightseers, while myriad roadside businesses dotted the highways to meet travelers' needs. As the twentieth century progressed, the boundaries between city and countryside would blur and, in some places, disappear.

On September 13, 1901, high in the Adirondack Mountains of New York State, a party of hikers paused for a picnic. For Theodore Roosevelt—rancher, sportsman, author, naturalist, and vice president of the United States—it was a welcome day of freedom. He had led his family on an energetic early-morning climb to the summit of Mount Marcy and now looked forward to a restful hour on the shores of Lake Tear of the Clouds. But, as the Roosevelts unpacked their lunch baskets, the peace of the autumn afternoon was shattered. A messenger, gasping for breath after his uphill run, brought grim news: The president of the United States was dying.

Seven days earlier, while visiting the Pan American Exposition in the burgeoning industrial city of Buffalo, New York, President William McKinley had been surrounded by a crowd of admirers, eager to shake the presidential hand. Yet among the crowd was one mentally unstable citizen who carried a gun concealed in a handkerchief. He shot McKinley at close range.

After the initial panic, the president's doctors had announced that, although the wound was serious, their patient would survive. They had reassured Vice President Roosevelt that there was no need to abandon his plans for a brief holiday in the Adirondacks. But they were wrong; McKinley was sinking fast, and by the time Roosevelt reached Buffalo, the president was dead. A few hours later, on the afternoon of September 14, 1901, Theodore Roosevelt took the oath of office, to become the twenty-sixth president of the United States.

The nation that Roosevelt received abruptly into his charge was in the throes of dramatic change. The men who had drafted the Constitution of the United States of America a dozen decades before could not have foreseen the transformation that awaited the tiny republic of farmers and frontiersmen. The thirteen original states along the Atlantic seaboard now represented a fraction of a continent-spanning behemoth, whose population of seventy-six million was growing by a million every year. Its wildernesses were tamed, its expanses trussed by the iron bands of the railways; its cities had burst their boundaries; its wealth had multiplied at a geometric rate; its industrialists not only waxed fat and powerful at home but gained an ever-greater share of markets overseas. From America's fields, mines, and wells now came half the world's cotton, wheat, copper, and oil, and one-third of its coal and gold.

By the time the new century began, the United States was reckoned the richest of nations: No other country on earth produced as much material wealth per capita. And no longer did this youthful giant look only inward: America had begun to flex its muscles and to pursue its own material interests by engaging in the power struggles of the world outside. In the first quarter of the twentieth century, the nation would continue to transform itself at a staggering speed.

This growth would be far from painless. Oil might gush from the earth, and new

Theodore Roosevelt gives a characteristically ebullient speech from behind a bench of scribbling New York reporters at a rally in 1911. With his political acuity and zest for life, Roosevelt embodied the virile spirit of the United States in the early twentieth century. As president from 1901 to 1909, he used his powers to force through social reforms, challenge the might of industry, and negotiate the Square Deal between labor and business. Roosevelt's foreign policy was equally vigorous: He shunned isolationism and involved the United States in world affairs as no president had done before.

inventions—such as the automobile—alter lives and landscapes beyond recognition, but people would die of poverty's diseases in the shadow of the magnates' mansions, the exploited and the unemployed would grow angry, and blood would flow in the streets. The underside of unregulated economic growth, and its human costs, would be exposed and challenged; laws would be passed to curb abuses and rectify ills. Debates would rage over the morality of big business, and the need—or otherwise—for federal intervention in the autonomous government of individual states. Racial discrimination, theoretically abolished after the Civil War of the preceding century, but rampant throughout the country—particularly in the rural South, where the majority of the black population lived—would become an increasingly visible problem. Old social values would be called into question, and new—some said dangerous—ideas explored. The generation that grew to maturity in the first quarter of the twentieth century would not look, think, or act like its parents and grandparents.

The fuel for some of this dynamism was fresh blood. Immigrants from all over Europe were pouring into the United States at an unprecedented rate. Between 1900 and 1910, some six million newcomers arrived, from the barren lands of southern Italy, from the bleak villages of Poland, from all the hungry and hopeless backwaters between Russia's Nizhni Novgorod and County Cork in Ireland. Some fled poverty or religious persecution, others craved brighter prospects than the Old World offered. America had earned a place in European folklore: Fishermen on the east coast of Scotland, for instance, nicknamed their richest fishing ground California, while the Jews of Latvia and Lithuania spoke longingly of the Golden Land across the sea.

The journey was not easily undertaken. Finding the money to book a passage was only the beginning. Would-be immigrants had to negotiate a bureaucratic obstacle course in pursuit of transit visas across European borders, identity cards, medical certificates, official verifications of taxes paid and military obligations fulfilled. Once the travelers reached the port of embarkation—be it Genoa, Liverpool, or Riga on the Baltic Sea—they might face a wait of weeks or even months until departure. This interlude could prove expensive: Some perspicacious boardinghouse owners were able to make their American fortunes without ever leaving home.

By the end of the nineteenth century, the price of a steerage ticket had fallen low enough to make the voyage possible even for people in relatively humble circumstances, and the fares now included food. (Earlier generations of immigrants had been forced to bring and cook their own provisions for the journey, which did nothing to ameliorate the cramped and noisome conditions belowdecks.) In 1900, steerage-class accommodations were still anything but luxurious, offering little privacy and only the most spartan of bunks and benches, but the crossing time was mercifully reduced, and steamships now traversed the Atlantic in just over a week.

By 1900, the United States had emerged as a world power. Its industries and open spaces were a magnet for immigrants seeking to escape the poverty and oppression of Europe. Most newcomers settled on the eastern seaboard (left), but cities of more than 500,000 existed even on the West Coast. Comprising forty-five states in 1900, the United States also owned Alaska—bought from Russia in 1867—and an empire (inset), won in a conflict with Spain over Cuba in 1898. Although most of these possessions soon gained their independence, in 1902, there were 60,000 troops in the Philippines.

Even after surviving the petty tyrannies of officials in their homelands, and the miseries of seasickness and claustrophobia on board, the aspiring immigrants faced an additional ordeal: the bewildering complex of waiting rooms, passageways, customs sheds, and dormitories on Ellis Island, the U.S. government reception center in New York Bay through

135

which three-quarters of all European immigrants entered the New World. Those who failed to satisfy the authorities as to their suitability to become American citizens were forced to turn around and undertake the grueling journey in reverse.

Throughout the nineteenth century, the majority of immigrants had come from the British Isles, Germany, and Scandinavia. But by the end of the century, the pattern had shifted. An ever-larger proportion of immigrants now came from southern and eastern Europe—from southern Italy, the Balkans, and the vast expanses of the Russian and Austro-Hungarian empires. On the West Coast, newcomers also arrived in increasing numbers from China, in spite of efforts on the part of some xenophobic politicians to have them barred entirely.

In the first ten years of the new century, three-fifths of all foreigners admitted were single adults, predominantly male, between the ages of fifteen and thirty-nine. Most of them were young and fit. And they would need to be. America might still be a land of opportunity, but its vast frontier territories were no longer free for the taking. Its industries might be avid for cheap labor, but its native workers were increasingly

Taking a break from politics, President Theodore Roosevelt gazes confidently into the camera as his horse clears a fence. Accomplished at sports and hunting, Roosevelt actively projected the image of an outdoorsman. He enjoyed shooting big game in Africa but also was a nature lover and conservationist, devoted to the untamed beauty of America's West. Campaigning vigorously to preserve the national heritage, he added 200,000 square miles to the country's national forests, established more than fifty reserves for wildlife, and designated the Grand Canyon a national monument.

jealous of their jobs: The trade unions of the day gave only the coolest of welcomes to foreign labor, or barred the immigrant from membership altogether. The work available was hard, ill-paid, and often dangerous: Roads, railways, and new houses were under construction as suburbs fanned out from the urban centers; harbors were dredged and expanded to meet the ever-growing needs of foreign trade; earth had to be dug and rock blasted for mine shafts, quarries, tunnels, gas pipes, and sewers.

Many European immigrants settled in the port cities and industrial communities of the Northeast, or in the towns that lay at the great railroad junctions farther inland: Buffalo, Cleveland, Pittsburgh, Chicago, Saint Louis, or Milwaukee. Most, seeking a haven of familiar language, foods, and faces in an otherwise incomprehensible land, gravitated to neighborhoods already settled by fellow expatriates. Italians gathered in New England and the Mid-Atlantic states, or crossed the continent to California in search of a climate like the one they had left behind, hospitable to vineyards and olive groves. Poles settled heavily in the Midwest, while the Jews from Russia and the Austro-Hungarian empire clustered in the cities of the eastern seaboard.

No matter where they came to rest, new arrivals with entrepreneurial instincts quickly carved out their own niches. Little capital outlay, and only the simplest of machinery, was needed to launch certain industries: On New York's teeming Lower East Side, for instance, virtually every tenement building hummed day and night with the sound of sewing machines as its inhabitants produced piecework for the garment trade. Those with the resources to do so set themselves up as peddlers, pushcart vendors, or small shopkeepers, often specializing in the products required by their particular communities: Italian bakers and kosher butchers, for example, met the demands of local and very familiar markets. Others provided services that no outsider could adequately supply: catering for social events and organizing funerals in accordance with the customs of the old country, or acting as brokers to send back money and gifts to relatives at home. A few set themselves up as local labor contractors, organizing their countrymen into work gangs and hiring them out for profit.

Not all migrants to the cities came from beyond America's borders. Poverty in the depressed farmlands of the South and the Midwest drove more and more country dwellers to seek work in the town. Many of these rural emigrants were black southerners who, desperate to escape the economic miseries and social rigidities of their home regions, looked to the cities to provide a way out of the trap.

Urban living conditions for poor newcomers, whatever their origins, were far from ideal to begin with, and worsened as new arrivals crowded into ramshackle tenements or jerry-built hovels owned by landlords happy to collect the rent but unenthusiastic about repairs. Rats ran in the airless alleyways, and nearly one out of five inhabitants could expect to die prematurely of one of poverty's diseases.

Slum housing in New York City was a public scandal. Journalist and urban reformer Jacob Riis, writing a few years before the new century began, shocked his readers with a description of the housing conditions to be found in one of the "dens of death" in the Mulberry Street Bend, a notorious Manhattan slum:

> In a room not thirteen feet either way slept twelve men and women, two or three in bunks set in a sort of alcove, the rest on the floor. A kerosene lamp burned dimly in the fearful atmosphere, probably to guide other and later arrivals to their "beds." . . . Most of the men were lodgers, who slept there for five cents a spot.

Some of the sleepers who crammed together in the Bend and places like it, dreaming their American dreams, would in time fight their way to something better. Every immigrant cherished the story of Andrew Carnegie, son of a penniless Scottish weaver, who had come to the United States as a ragged urchin and plied his wits to garner one of the world's greatest fortunes, as master of the American steel industry. But for most, the gulf between themselves and the Carnegies of the land could hardly be wider. The founders of the republic may have envisioned a country free of domineering kings and princes. But America in 1900 possessed its own aristocracy, a ruling class not of blood, but of corporate wealth. The barons of commerce and industry wielded more power, and lived more grandly, than any of their medieval counterparts in the vanished feudal world across the water.

Business was booming. It was a time of widespread prosperity, at least for those who had already found or been born into their places in the economic mainstream. And none were more prosperous than the developers of railways, the men who mined the country's seemingly inexhaustible mineral wealth, the industrialists who turned it into iron or steel, and the financiers who bankrolled these enterprises.

A potent blend of talent, luck, and commercial acumen, plus an immunity to excessive sentiment or scruple, had brought men like banker J. P. Morgan and oil king John D. Rockefeller into positions of unprecedented strength. Rising in an era when state and federal governments hesitated to impose any curbs on economic freedom, these magnates enjoyed a degree of influence that any mere politician would envy. And, like any traditional aristocracy, these men of business forged bonds and alliances to protect their common interests. They sat on the boards of one another's companies, provided the backing for one another's ventures, and manipulated competition by combining against upstarts and outsiders. Morgan and his business partners, for instance, held more than 300 directorships in twelve public-utility companies, thirty-four banks, ten major insurance houses, twenty-four manufacturing and trading corporations, and thirty-two transportation firms.

Industrialists and their financial backers collaborated to drive out competition and dominate their particular markets. They created powerful monopolies, controlling costs and supplies of raw materials, setting rock-bottom wage levels, and fixing prices high enough to guarantee spectacular profits. If some independent entrepreneur dared to venture into their territory—perhaps with the ambition of offering consumers better quality and lower prices—he would be stamped out with cold-blooded efficiency. Popularly known as the trusts, these secretive organizations had the resources to buy friends in high places. State and federal legislation either served their interests, or had a way of getting lost somewhere between enactment and enforcement.

By the turn of the century, a growing body of public opinion had begun to view these giants with alarm. Social and political reform was in the air. The middle classes, while enjoying their share of the national prosperity, sensed that all was not as it should be. It was time, they felt, for the federal government to flex its muscles and curb the abuses perpetrated by the strong against the weak. Their work was not easy. Lincoln Steffens, one of the first of a generation of crusading journalists known as muckrakers, described his efforts to investigate corruption in local politics:

> *Every time I attempted to trace to its sources the political corruption of a city ring, the stream of corruption branched off in the most unexpected directions, and spread out in a network of veins and arteries so complex*

GATEWAY TO THE NEW WORLD

For prospective Americans such as those depicted below, the view of the Statue of Liberty was cause for jubilation. Next to this symbol of hope, however, lay Ellis Island, the receiving station where immigrants' aspirations might yet be dashed.

Having docked at Hudson River Pier, passengers boarded a ferry to Ellis Island. In the depot's reception hall, their generally meager baggage was held while they were shepherded upstairs to the Registry Hall. There they faced a two-tier inspection designed to determine their eligibility for citizenship. Asked to wait in a labyrinth of pens and gangways, they underwent a thorough medical examination before a registration inspector interviewed them about their occupation, solvency, and politics. Most immigrants were processed in less than a day and were ferried to Manhattan; others were held longer as their status was investigated; and a few—mainly paupers and criminals—were deported.

Since its opening in 1892, Ellis Island had been the filter through which 70 percent of immigrants passed before embarking on their new lives. After the peak years at the beginning of the century, the gates to the New World narrowed with each new piece of legislation. And after quotas set drastic curbs on immigration in 1921 and 1924, the flood of humanity passing through Ellis Island dwindled to a trickle.

Laden with baggage, an Italian family leaves the ferry that has carried them to Ellis Island. Apprehension that they might fail the subsequent medical examination and be deported led many immigrants to dub the place "Heartbreak Island."

During the early years of the century, a kaleidoscope of hopefuls reached the new shore, increasingly coming from troubled lands in southern and eastern Europe. Later legislation, however, limited annual entry to two percent of ethnic stocks already present in 1890.

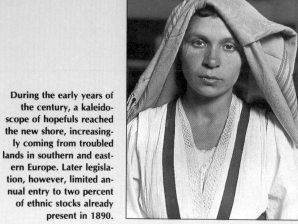

An Albanian woman wears national garb.

Fatigue hoods an Armenian Jew's eyes.

Age seams a Czech woman's face.

A uniformed inspector carefully examines the eyes of a would-be American citizen. At the ports of departure, immigrants were issued a certificate of good health. Even so, on arrival in America, they had to undergo a rigorous medical examination for communicable diseases. Trachoma, a blinding ailment, was one of the most common reasons for medical detention.

Travel-weary immigrants crowd the iron pens of Ellis Island's cavernous Registry Hall following a mental-health inspection. Legislation passed in 1907 forbade the entry of those with mental deficiencies that might prevent them from earning a living.

Ethnic jewelry adorns a Syrian Muslim.

A stowaway Finn stares with resignation.

that hardly any part of the body politic seemed clear. It flowed out of politics into vice and crime, out of politics into business, and back again into politics. . . . A system is in control of the land.

Some muckrakers turned their attentions to specific industries. Journalist Ida Tarbell compiled a three-volume history of Rockefeller's Standard Oil Company, a well-documented dossier of double-dealing, chicanery, and strong-arm tactics. The appalling lack of sanitation and horrendous working conditions in the Chicago meat-packing industry, exposed in *The Jungle,* a novel by Upton Sinclair, nauseated the American public and inspired the United States Congress to draft a stringent Pure Food and Drug Act.

Into this bracing political climate came the youngest American president to date. Theodore Roosevelt was six weeks short of his forty-third birthday when he took the oath of office. His admirers extolled his vigor, bravado, and progressive zeal: No leader was better suited to steer the country into the dawning century. Others were less enthusiastic. Mark Hanna, national chairman of Roosevelt's own party, made no secret of his dismay: "Now that damned cowboy is in the White House!"

The tag of cowboy might have seemed incongruous for the Harvard-educated scion of one of New York State's wealthy old Dutch families. But Roosevelt had overcome a sickly childhood to become a robust, sports-loving outdoorsman. Shortly after graduation, he had used a portion of his inherited riches to purchase a ranch in the wild northern territory of the Dakotas. At first, his cowhands had mocked his eastern accent and patrician style, but soon realized that their boss, working alongside them in all weather on the range, was no mere city slicker. "He wasn't a purty

Standing at the remote testing ground of Kill Devil Hills in North Carolina, aviation pioneer Wilbur Wright looks on as his brother Orville makes history in the world's first manned, powered, and sustained flight. The ingredients for flight—advances in aerodynamics, structural engineering, fuel technology, and engine development—were already in existence. It remained only for the Wright brothers to combine them in a practical machine. Years spent watching the flight of birds and hundreds of experiments with gliders culminated on December 17, 1903, when the Wrights' biplane, powered by a lightweight engine and propellers, took to the air and traveled 852 feet in fifty-nine seconds.

Soaring to 800 feet, the Woolworth Building dwarfs its Manhattan neighbors. Erected by architect Cass Gilbert in 1913 as the headquarters for Frank W. Woolworth's chain-store empire, the Gothic-style Cathedral of Commerce, as it was later nicknamed, remained for seventeen years the tallest structure in the world. What made the time ripe for building such an edifice was the availability of inexpensive steel for girders and other structural elements, and newly efficient elevators for whisking the occupants up and down.

rider, but he was a hell of a good rider," acknowledged one of his cowboys.

The demands of ranching consumed only a fraction of Roosevelt's prodigious energy. He carved out a career as a writer and historian—indeed, he had completed his first published work, a history of the War of 1812, while still an undergraduate. Biographies, narratives of hunting trips and cowboy life, and a best-selling account of the conquest of the American West flowed from his pen. Yet his principal passion was politics. In 1882, at the age of twenty-three, he was elected to the New York State legislature, where he rapidly made his mark as a reformer, sponsoring or supporting bills for factory safety and improved working conditions.

Moving from the legislature into a series of appointed posts, as head of the Civil Service Commission and president of the New York Board of Police Commissioners, he gained a reputation as an enemy of all forms of corruption and an advocate of fair-employment practices. He swept away the old system of distributing plum jobs to political cronies and the party faithful, in favor of a system of examinations for public posts. As a dedicated supporter of women's rights, he opened to female applicants a range of civil-service occupations previously limited to men. In 1897, he was brought into the federal government as assistant secretary of the U.S. Navy, just in time for a pugnacious episode that would turn him into a national hero.

Tensions were mounting in the Caribbean, as relations between the United States and Spain, the region's dominant imperial power, rapidly deteriorated. The main bone of contention was the sugar-growing island of Cuba. For 400 years, it had been a Spanish colony, part of a once-large empire in the Americas and the Pacific Ocean, but a growing independence movement now sought to throw off the imperial yoke. In the United States, public opinion—fueled by a campaign in the popular press—was firmly in favor of a Spanish withdrawal. Spanish rule had been harsh, but American support for a Cuban revolution was not founded solely on humanitarian grounds. The United States had invested heavily in the island's economy, and a free Cuba made good financial sense to its northern backers.

An opportunity to safeguard that investment came on February 15, 1898. While paying an allegedly friendly visit to Cuba's harbor capital, Havana, the battleship USS *Maine* blew up, with the loss of 266 men. The cause of the explosion was never ascertained, but a U.S. Navy court of inquiry was quick to pin the blame on a Spanish mine, and in mid-April, the United States went to war. A naval blockade was set up to help the Cuban insurgents, and preparations were made for the landing of U.S. troops. A decisive victory for the invaders in July, at the battle of San Juan Hill, was accompanied by the defeat of Spain's two flotillas off the port of Santiago de Cuba and near the Philippine capital of Manila, and within four months, the fighting was over. It had been, in the words of Theodore Roosevelt, "a splendid little war."

And much of the splendor rubbed off on Roosevelt himself, who, inspired by the Cuban cause, had resigned his post at the Navy Department and handpicked a volunteer regiment of cavalry, known as the Rough Riders. This valiant but unconventional band of Dakota cowboys, American Indians, New York City mounted policemen, and college football stars fought its way to fame and victory at the battle of San Juan Hill. The actual winning of the war may have had more to do with the strength of the U.S. Navy than with military action on Cuban soil, but in the minds of the American public, "Teddy" and his Rough Riders were the heroes of the hour.

In 1898, Roosevelt was elected governor of New York State. He remained in office scarcely a year before answering his party's call to serve as President McKinley's

A PASSAGE TO THE PACIFIC

NORTH AMERICA

PANAMA

Caribbean Sea

• Colón

• Panama

0   20
MILES

Gulf of Panama

Caribbean Sea

Atlantic Ocean

Pacific Ocean

SOUTH AMERICA

Passing under a rocky bluff, the USS *Ohio* is towed through the Panama Canal's Culebra Cut in 1915. In constructing the ten-mile cut, the canal builders used 100 steam shovels, 4,000 wagons, and 280 locomotives to literally move mountains. Hills, peaks, and ridges were lowered—some by as much as 300 feet—to create a 500-foot-wide channel running 85 feet above sea level. Conditions were arduous; one steam-shovel operator dubbed the cut "Hell's Gorge." At noon, the temperature in the bottom of the cut could reach 120° F.: Volatile dynamite and frequent mud slides killed many workers. Dredging was still going on when, at 11:15 a.m. on August 15, 1914, the freighter *Ancon* entered the cut on the canal's formal opening.

For centuries, seafarers making the arduous, 8,000-mile journey around South America had envisaged a canal cutting across the mountainous Isthmus of Panama to link the Pacific and Atlantic oceans. In 1914, the dream was finally realized through the dogged determination of Theodore Roosevelt.

First, however, a fiasco occurred. Construction of a sea-level waterway was started in 1881, by a French company led by Ferdinand de Lesseps, builder of the Suez Canal, which linked the Mediterranean and the Red Sea. Ten years, 28,000 deaths, and hundreds of millions of francs later, the French admitted defeat. Bad planning, tropical disease, and machinery unequal to the task all contributed to the company's demise. Roosevelt, alert to the strategic importance of the canal, acquired the company's assets and rights to build. Obstruction from the Colombian government, which demanded more than 100 million dollars for the right to build on its territory, was overcome by a timely uprising covertly encouraged by the United States. In 1903, for only one-tenth of the original asking price, the United States was granted a ten-mile-wide canal zone (inset, left) in perpetuity by the new Republic of Panama.

Three years later, work commenced on a fifty-mile, high-level canal, incorporating locks and existing lakes in place of Lesseps's sea-level design. At the peak period of construction, the labor force totaled 85,000 men. Their greatest challenge was the Culebra Cut at the highest point on the isthmus. Improved medical knowledge, military-style organization, state-of-the-art technology, and a budget of 352 million dollars ensured success.

The finished structure consisted of three pairs of locks that raised ships eighty-five feet above sea level. Lake water replaced the sixty million gallons that descended to the sea with each ship's passage.

running mate in his 1900 bid for reelection. Roosevelt provided much-needed balance for the Republican ticket: McKinley, in his first presidential term, had acquired the reputation of being the friend, if not the puppet, of big business; it was hoped that Roosevelt, with his progressive image, could prevent reform-minded Republicans from switching their loyalties to the opposition.

Big-business interests breathed a sigh of relief when McKinley won a second term. After the assassin's bullet catapulted Roosevelt into the presidency, the captains of industry hoped that he would continue his predecessor's policy of leaving them more or less alone to pursue their corporate fortunes. But they were in for a shock.

Barely a year into his presidency, Roosevelt outraged the capitalist barons by invoking the Sherman Antitrust Act against Northern Securities, one of many apparently independent companies controlled, behind the scenes, by J. P. Morgan and a consortium of other, equally powerful tycoons. This legislation, enacted in 1890, had been intended to prevent industrial combinations and monopolies from conspiring to control or restrain trade. But in the decade after its passage, the only successful prosecutions under the act had been directed against labor unions rather than business interests. Now Roosevelt turned this weapon against the Morgan empire, charging it with the creation of a transportation monopoly, the flotation of stock of dubious value at inflated prices, and the imposition of extortionate charges on the public at large, resulting in exaggerated profits for the operators. The Detroit Free Press observed that "Wall Street is paralyzed at the thought that a president of the United States would sink so low as to try to enforce the law." Morgan himself was heard to complain to a party of dinner guests that Roosevelt was "not a gentleman."

Other ungentlemanly actions followed. In a bitter dispute between the coal companies and the miners, Roosevelt not only refused the mine operators' request to send in federal troops against the strikers but set up an arbitration commission and—worse—acknowledged that the miners' unions had the right to negotiate on their members' behalf. The miners went back to work, and their employers agreed to improve pay and some working conditions, in return for a 10 percent raise in the price of coal. The settlement, giving equal consideration to the needs of business and of organized labor, exemplified what Roosevelt dubbed his policy of the Square Deal.

In one area, however, the president was unequivocally partisan: He was a passionate conservationist, deeply committed to the protection of the country's natural resources and determined to stop wholesale depredations of the landscape in the name of profits. During his eight-year administration, he established national parks and forests, promoted bills to finance irrigation and land reclamation, protected the timberlands from wholesale devastation by private lumber syndicates, and established controls over dam building and the use of harbors and waterways.

In an address delivered in the final year of his presidency, he observed that "in the past we have admitted the right of the individual to injure the future of the republic for his own present profit. The time has come for a change. As a people we have the right and the duty . . . to protect ourselves and our children against the wasteful development of our natural resources."

The expression of such sentiments, in a society where the right to pursue profit was frequently deemed more sacred than any of the freedoms enshrined in the Constitution, alarmed industrialists. Yet Roosevelt was unpredictable. He was as likely to block one reform as he was to promulgate another. And he displayed considerable ambivalence toward the revelations of muckraking journalists—responding wholeheartedly to their battle cries one day, excoriating their negativism the next.

Roosevelt's presidential style was that of a maverick: He was reluctant to delegate major initiatives to the appropriate cabinet departments or to wait for Congress to approve his actions. As on San Juan Hill, he liked to lead the charge himself.

Nowhere was this dogged individualism more evident than in Roosevelt's handling of foreign affairs. He came to the presidency at a time when the United States found itself playing a new role on the world stage: that of a significant global power, with an empire of its own. Imperial status, in fact, had been almost accidental. Victory in the Spanish-American War not only had brought Cuba independence but also had given the American government direct control over other former Spanish possessions—Puerto Rico, the Pacific island of Guam, and the archipelago of the Philippines. Many Americans were reluctant to take up the imperial mantle; the memory of their own liberation struggle against Britain was still comparatively green.

But the United States could not neglect its huge, and growing, economic involvements in the Americas, the Far East, and elsewhere. And where the nation's purse led, its political attention followed. Roosevelt wished to see the United States as a global peacemaker, moral leader, and exemplar of the democratic way of life. If American influence on the world scene brought financial gain, so much the better.

In China, for instance, Britain, France, Germany, and Russia had forced the weak Qing dynasty to open the country to foreign investment and trade, and were jockeying for control over major ports and waterways. Roosevelt, believing that the Chinese empire offered spectacular commercial opportunities, was determined to share in the bonanza without compromising his moral stance. He espoused the doctrine known as the Open Door policy, committing the United States to defend Chinese sovereignty over its own territories in exchange for equal access to the large, potentially lucrative Chinese market.

To take full advantage of opportunities in the Far East, the United States needed better access to the Pacific Ocean. Pressure mounted for a canal through Panama—the narrow isthmus of Colombian territory that linked Central and South America. The benefits to domestic as well as foreign trade were readily apparent: By cutting out the long and dangerous passage around Cape Horn, the waterway would radically reduce the cost and time of a sea journey between the two seaboards, and simplify the movements of all international shipping between the hemispheres. As the dominant economic power in the Americas, the United States took control of the development.

Reluctant to leave matters in the care of professional diplomats, Roosevelt launched into personal negotiations with the Colombian government. When that country's leaders proved uncooperative, a revolt broke out in the proposed canal zone, and a party of insurgents declared Panama's independence. Roosevelt rapidly offered recognition to the rebel republic and pursued his discussions with the new proprietors. Later, he denied accusations that he had fomented the uprising: "I did not lift my finger to incite the revolutionists . . . I simply ceased to stamp out the different revolutionary fuses that were already burning."

For every observer left aghast at Roosevelt's buccaneering style of diplomacy, there were others who admired his personal interventions. Indeed, he was awarded the Nobel Peace Prize in 1906 for his prominent role in negotiating an end to the bitter war between Russia and Japan.

Nevertheless, the president was not averse to a show of his own country's military power. During his administration, the United States Navy was improved, expanded,

Members of New York's 69th Infantry Regiment enthusiastically kiss their sweethearts good-bye in August 1917, as they leave for the battlefields of Europe. When President Wilson declared war on Germany in April of that year, the U.S. Army numbered barely 200,000 badly trained and ill-equipped volunteers. Conscription, introduced in May, eventually increased the number of troops to four million, swamping the training camps with raw recruits. Initially, weapons and uniforms were in short supply: Many men trained in civilian clothes with broomsticks for rifles. But the nearly two million doughboys who landed in France between March and October of 1918 proved themselves an effective military force whose presence made a significant contribution to the Allied victory.

and sent on a world tour as a display of American strength, especially directed toward those parts of the Far East where the United States was anxious to affirm its trading rights and to ensure that the Open Door stayed open. He made no secret of his credo: "I never take a step in foreign policy unless I am assured that I shall be able eventually to carry out my will by force."

At home, Roosevelt's progressivism had its limits. His reputation for fairness was tarnished during an outbreak of racial tension on a Texas army base in 1906. Although both black and white soldiers served in the United States Army, they did so in separate companies. Certain members of one all-black unit were accused of murdering a white bartender in a saloon outside the camp. No culprits were positively identified, and no trial was ever held. On suspicion that the soldiers were covering up for their comrades, the president ordered the wholesale punishment of three black companies at the fort. All 160 members of these companies—including men who had won medals for bravery in battle and lifelong veterans on the verge of retirement—were dishonorably discharged. Critics questioned whether a group of white soldiers would have been treated in the same manner. But in spite of such stains on his record, Roosevelt's popularity remained undiminished.

When Roosevelt chose not to run for reelection in 1908, he withdrew from the limelight to occupy himself with African safaris and other unpresidential pleasures. His successor, fellow Republican William Howard Taft, possessed none of Roosevelt's charisma, although, at a weight of more than 300 pounds, he made up in girth what he lacked in political glamour. Taft, a former judge, had served in Roosevelt's cabinet as secretary of war but had never held any elective office until he reached the presidency.

Taft's critics found him markedly impervious to the spirit of the age: The urge for social reform, the revulsion felt by many citizens for the worst abuses of big business and the trusts, the growing demands for social justice, all seemed to have passed him by. Kansas newspaper editor William Allen White, a prominent observer of the contemporary American scene, deemed the president "as insensible of public opinion and the currents of public thought as an oriental satrap."

Invited to address the National American Women's Suffrage Association, campaigners on behalf of citizens still denied the vote on grounds of gender, Taft infuriated his audience by claiming that most women were not interested in the right to vote. If they were enfranchised, he declared, power would flow into the hands of females "of the less desirable class." The suffragists virtually hissed him off the stage.

Despite Taft's apparent indifference to progressive causes, significant reforms reached the statute books during his term of office. Employees on federal projects were, for the first time, guaranteed an eight-hour day; controls were imposed on corporations' contributions to political campaigns; a separate Department of Labor was added to the federal government; the previous administration's Pure Food and Drug Act was strengthened. Government lawyers continued to harry the trusts and enforce the law; more-effective legislation was introduced to control interstate commerce and the running of the railways. And, to the fury of the very rich, the Sixteenth Amendment to the Constitution was ratified at the very end of Taft's four-year term, giving the federal government the right to impose an income tax.

The country as a whole continued to wax fat. But the gulf between rich and poor seemed greater than ever. It was estimated that a mere seventy Americans now controlled one-sixteenth of the total national wealth, and exploitation of the lowest ranks of the labor force persisted. In 1911, for instance, the nation was horrified by a fire at the Triangle Shirtwaist Factory, one of the innumerable sweatshops that made up New York City's enormous garment industry. The factory managers had locked the exit doors on the upper stories, to prevent their employees from leaving their machines to use the toilets on the outside landings. Hundreds of young women, mostly eastern European immigrants, were forced to jump from the factory windows, with skirts and hair ablaze: 146 of them died.

Through a legal technicality, the Triangle owners were acquitted of any responsibility for the disaster, but the subsequent public outcry led to the strengthening of regulations for factory safety and building control. The tragedy also gave impetus to a campaign for better working conditions, spearheaded by the International Ladies' Garment Workers' Union.

Support for specific causes coalesced into a general crusade for reform. It was an overwhelmingly middle-class movement, whose members applied themselves to the

Photographed in 1918 from atop a seventy-foot-high tower, 21,000 enlisted men and officers form a monumental portrait of President Woodrow Wilson at an Ohio army training camp. A man of high ideals, Wilson had won the 1916 election campaigning for peace. German aggression caused him to abandon his neutral stance in 1917 and bring the United States into the war on the side of the Allies. Nevertheless, his vision of the conflict as a crusade "for the ultimate peace of the world and for the liberation of its peoples" was to strongly influence the postwar division of Europe and the subsequent formation of the League of Nations.

struggle with methodical efficiency and missionary zeal. Theirs was not a cry for radical change or socialist revolution, but a demand that every American should share in the fruits of prosperity. "Discontent," remarked William Allen White, "has shaved its whiskers, washed its shirt, and put on a derby hat."

Activists on many different fronts came together to form a new political party that would challenge the Republican and Democratic duopoly in the presidential contest of 1912. The Progressive party, popularly known as the Bull Moose Progressives, was a broad church indeed, attracting rich industrialists of liberal inclinations as well as veteran warriors for social justice. "Think of me and Jane Addams on the same platform!" mused one of J. P. Morgan's old business associates, when he found

149

The Dry Years

At midnight on January 16, 1920, following persistent campaigning by the temperance movement, the Eighteenth Amendment banned the manufacture and sale of intoxicating drinks.

Alcohol remained available to individuals with initiative. Armed with a library book, a portable still from the hardware store, and some potato peels, citizens could brew a bracing drink for just a few dollars. A rapidly soaring number of "patients" arrived at drugstores with prescriptions for medicinal alcohol. Illicit drinking clubs catered to the rich: By 1925, New York City boasted several thousand such speakeasies, supplied by bootleggers and "protected" by racketeers.

Manufacturers, too, found a way around the law. California vintners produced a grape juice, called Vine-Glo, that turned into wine if fermented properly. Brewers sold near beer, a low-alcohol concoction that could be mixed with yeast to become "nearer" still.

The task of those appointed to enforce the law may have seemed futile. Among the poor, however, alcohol consumption decreased and large parts of the United States did become truly dry. Despite this modest success, increasing gangland violence brought disillusionment among Prohibition's supporters. On December 5, 1933, the amendment was repealed and the drought ended.

Under the eye of the police, a cask of wine is consigned to New York's sewers in the early 1920s. Unaware of the violence about to blight what they saw as a "noble experiment," many Americans anticipated an era of clean living and clear thinking.

himself sitting side by side with the pioneering social worker from Chicago's slums.

Theodore Roosevelt returned to public life to take up the banner for the cause and became the new party's presidential candidate. In a rousing speech to the party in June 1912, he declared: "We stand at Armageddon, and we battle for the Lord!" Outside, the streets were mobbed with supporters shouting "We want Teddy!"

But in the particular Armageddon of the 1912 election, the advocates of the new reforming center party failed in their crusade. Progressive Republicans, unimpressed with the apparent conservatism of incumbent President Taft, did move their votes to the new ticket. Progressive Democrats, however, resisted Teddy Roosevelt's charisma, stayed loyal to their own, more left-leaning party, and won the day.

The winner was an unlikely figure to emerge victorious from the cut-and-thrust of an American presidential contest. Woodrow Wilson, former president of Princeton University, was an intellectual. A lifelong student of the science of government, he had not stepped into the smoke-filled rooms of electoral politics until the age of fifty-four, and found himself in the White House just over two years later.

Wilson, bred in the southern state of Virginia, was the son, nephew, and grandson of Presbyterian ministers. An early interest in public affairs and the practicalities of government was channeled into an academic career: "I knew very well," Wilson

later admitted, "that a man without an independent fortune must in any case content himself with becoming an outside force in politics."

So articulate was this outside force, however, that Wilson gained considerable fame, both as a commentator on politics for serious journals and as a college president dedicated to reforming the patrician institution in his charge. He was originally viewed as a fairly conservative progressive, who spoke of his aspirations for the Democratic party as "a party of conservative reform, acting in the spirit of law and of ancient institutions." He hesitated to display partisanship in the continuing struggles between big business and organized labor. "We can't abolish the trusts," he insisted; "we must moralize them."

But by the time Wilson entered the political arena as gubernatorial candidate for the state of New Jersey in 1910, he had moved perceptibly toward the left. Some commentators suggested that his arguments with the wealthy graduates who held the purse strings at Princeton had disillusioned him once and for all about the rich. He was supported in his campaign by New Jersey's notoriously corrupt Democratic machine but, once elected, turned his back on the party bosses. One of his first acts as governor was to reform the legislation that had made New Jersey a haven for the powerful trusts and large corporations that wished to operate unhindered by state control or public scrutiny.

Federal agents stand beside the paraphernalia of a confiscated still in a suburban backyard. Only 2,000 agents were appointed to enforce the law, and corruption was rife. In 1925, agents seized eight million gallons of illicit alcohol—fewer than were drunk.

His achievements in New Jersey made Wilson a frontrunner for the Democratic presidential nomination. His hopes for America were expressed with missionary zeal: "I am interested in nothing so much as releasing the energy of the country." He proposed to achieve this by releasing the economy from the suffocating grip of the trusts, to let fresh air into the system and create a climate where new ventures and small enterprises could thrive without fear of destruction by the corporate giants.

His sincerity impressed the voters, and although his views on many reforms were not radically different from those espoused by Roosevelt and the Bull Moose Progressives, the split in right-of-center ranks carried Wilson into the presidency. The public greeted him with goodwill. "Mr. Wilson is the best listener that has been in the White House for many a year," remarked journalist William Hale. "Mr. Roosevelt never listened to anybody in his life, of course; Mr. Taft could listen well, when interested, but people often suspected that Mr. Taft's mind was a-wandering."

On some issues, Wilson seemed to have listened well. He rapidly launched into reforms of tariffs and taxation, and overhauled the banking system. He helped create a climate where unprecedented change seemed possible. Early in his presidency, and with his wholehearted support, all United States Senators were persuaded to make a public declaration of their personal financial and commercial interests. Earlier generations of American politicians, who had often regarded the Senate as a legitimate vehicle for feathering their own nests, would have been astonished to see their successors obediently lining up before the committee of inquiry to enumerate their stocks and shares and real-estate investments.

Yet some progressives complained that the new president's committment to reform was only skin-deep. They perceived a reluctance to come to grips with some of the more burning social problems of the day, and were disappointed in the administration's apparent lack of motivation on such issues as the reform of child labor laws, government aid to the unemployed, and racial discrimination. Indeed, segregation took a firmer hold during Wilson's administration, when previously unsegregated government departments were restructured to separate black and white staff.

Throughout the country, the cauldron of unrest began to boil. Fierce labor disputes broke out in many industries. None was more bitter than the fifteen-month battle between the United Mine Workers union and the Rockefeller-owned mining companies in the western state of Colorado. The miners, mostly ill-paid immigrant laborers from southern and central Europe, lived with their families in settlements of company-owned houses, where the mine managers' word was law. They were compelled to use only company-owned shops and company doctors, and forbidden to organize union meetings or political discussions. Company spies and strong-arm men made sure these rules were obeyed. Working conditions were dangerous: Between 1886 and 1913, more than seven workers out of every thousand died in accidents in the mine.

In September 1913, the miners launched a strike. Evicted from their homes, they set up tents and lived under canvas throughout the winter of 1913-1914. The management's private army of

Crowds goggle at 40,000 white-robed members of the Ku Klux Klan marching down Washington's Pennsylvania Avenue on their first national parade in August 1925. A southern vigilante group, originally formed to persecute blacks after the Civil War in the previous century, the Klan was disbanded in 1869 but enjoyed a nationwide rebirth in 1915. By the early 1920s, its slogan Native, White, Protestant Supremacy had attracted a membership of more than three million, drawn mainly from rural communities. As the self-proclaimed defender of traditional American values, the Klan terrorized its victims—blacks, Catholics, Jews, and foreigners—with lynchings, brandings, and burnings.

Sporting a knee-length coat and short, bobbed hair under a stylish hat, a young New Yorker steps out of her gleaming automobile. Having won the vote in 1920, fashionable young women—known as flappers, possibly after fledgling birds trying their wings—flaunted their freedom in ways that often shocked the older generation. Raised hems and light-colored stockings were just two manifestations of the flappers' vigorous assertion of their right to independence and pleasure. They smoked and drank in public, talked freely about sex, and saw Freudian analysts. As women of all classes entered the work force in growing numbers, the privileged young flappers stood as a beacon of female emancipation.

strikebreakers harassed the miners, disrupted their picket lines, and menaced their families. The mine owners refused to negotiate with the union, and asked the governor of Colorado to call out the state militia and declare martial law. In April 1914, the troops, armed with machine guns, launched a cavalry charge against the tent city, shot into the ensuing melee, and set the canvas shelters on fire. Forty-five people were killed, including two women and eleven children.

The strike failed when the union ran out of money. The owners stood firm, aware that there were plenty of workers desperate enough to accept low pay and dangerous conditions. Despite public outrage, such incidents were to become commonplace. As Walter Lippmann, editor of the liberal journal the *New Republic,* observed, "Here in America, life is extraordinarily cheap. There is almost no task so dull, so degrading, or so useless but you can find plenty of human beings to do it."

The widespread hunger for work, of any kind, was symptomatic: By 1914, the United States languished in an economic depression. For a major cause of the crisis, Americans had to look beyond their own shores: Europe was plunging into war. Britain, France, and Germany—three of America's best customers for its exports—were diverting all their resources to the war effort. In New York, the stock market reeled under a succession of financial panics. The cotton farmers of the South, primary suppliers to the European textile industry, faced ruin. On the waterfronts, dockworkers, merchant seamen, and the armies of clerks from the import and export houses lost their jobs. As the effects of the slump spread through the system, the construction industry also suffered, and with it the suppliers of timber, iron, and steel. In industrial communities throughout the nation, families stood in bread lines; the more public-spirited members of the affluent classes made donations to assist the poor and staffed soup kitchens. In the eastern city of Philadelphia, approximately 50 percent of the working population was unemployed, hunger marchers took to the streets in Chicago, and one-fifth of all Bostonians were dependent on municipal relief funds.

Within a year, the crisis ended in some areas. As America's old European customers returned, this time to buy war matériel, some regions and industries even experienced a boom. In the agricultural Midwest, farmers were blessed with a better harvest than they had enjoyed for years. The United States now had surplus food to sell to countries whose farms had turned into battlefields. Over the next two years, exports to Europe would virtually triple.

At first, President Wilson tried to avoid taking sides in the conflict across the Atlantic. In 1914, he issued an official proclamation stating that the United States would remain neutral, and called upon American citizens to keep an open mind. Military officers were forbidden to engage in any public discussion of the war.

But it proved impossible for the United States to maintain its lofty distance from the fight. American merchant shipping was caught in the cross fire: The British blockaded U.S. vessels carrying food to Germany, while German submarines harried American vessels as well as those of their official enemies, England and France. Public opinion swung strongly against Germany when the liner *Lusitania* was sunk by a German submarine in May 1915, with a loss of 1,200 innocent lives—128 of them American.

Little publicity was given at the time to the fact that the steamship was also carrying American-made ammunition for Allied guns.

Throughout the nation the quarrel raged: Should the United States take its place alongside the Allied forces to fight the Central Powers—Germany, the Austro-Hungarian empire, and Turkey? Americans' opinions were as diverse as their origins. The wealthy, well-educated East Coast establishment, predominantly white, Anglo-Saxon, and Protestant with strong cultural ties to Britain, was heavily in favor of joining the Allies. Those of Irish stock hated the English, and scorned the notion of going to war on their behalf. Central European immigrants sympathized with the cause of their Austro-Hungarian homeland. Russian Jews, while hating the czar, feared for the safety of their kinfolk at home, forcibly conscripted into the Russian army. Nor was all opposition based on ethnic loyalties. Quakers and secular pacifists argued against involvement on moral grounds, while socialists and anarchists maintained that the entire conflict was merely a capitalist exercise, and no member of the working class should become a pawn in the plutocrats' game. The greater the distance from the Atlantic, the stronger the antiwar sentiment seemed to be: Dwellers in the midwestern heartland and the Far West were more inclined than their eastern compatriots to favor a neutral stance.

Wilson hesitated, asserting that the United States should be too proud to fight, but ex-President Roosevelt roared from the sidelines that it was time to go to war. Finally, in 1917, with German submarines sinking U.S. shipping indiscriminately, Wilson decided that the Central Powers had to be stopped. He brought the United States into the war on the Allied side, vowing to make the world safe for democracy.

In May 1917, the president signed the Selective Service Act, establishing military conscription, and on the appointed registration day, more than nine million young men put their names down for the draft. Early in the summer, a lottery was held to choose the 687,000 names for the first intake of soldiers. The government launched a massive building program to construct army camps to house the draftees, and small towns held parades, with flags and marching bands, to send off their youth as local heroes. A wave of anti-German sentiment swept the nation: Schools banned the German language from the curriculum, patriotically minded music lovers smashed their Bach and Beethoven recordings, restaurants rewrote their menus to offer Salisbury Steak and Liberty Cabbage instead of hamburgers and sauerkraut. German immigrants, or those suspected of German origins, were attacked and sometimes lynched, without a pause to inquire into their political opinions.

In Washington, Wilson put the war effort on a systematic footing, appointing financier Bernard Baruch to mobilize the economy as head of the new War Industries Board. The message was broadcast: "He serves best who saves most." To help the war effort, raw materials had to be conserved and waste eradicated. No detail was too small for the board's attention: Its officials even compelled manufacturers to reduce the height of women's high-heeled shoes—the leather thus saved was required for cavalry harnesses and officers' belts. The consumer would have to put up, for patriotic reasons, with a much-reduced freedom of choice; the number of different pocketknives on the market, for instance, was lowered from 6,000 to 100.

The United States was at war for nineteen months, until the armistice of November 1918. In that short period, it spent ten times more than it had on the Civil War. It also paid a high cost in human life, although with only 320,710 deaths, the nation got off more lightly than its fellow combatants, whose casualties topped eight million.

President Wilson, committed to reshaping a shattered Europe in accordance with his democratic ideals, traveled to France to take part in the peace negotiations. Like Roosevelt before him, he chose to depart from the conventional rituals of diplomacy by taking charge of the delegation himself. But he held no brief for amateurism: In his entourage came hundreds of experts—academics and others—to advise him on the ethnography, history, and economy of Europe.

At the negotiating table, Wilson put forward a far-reaching peace plan. Its centerpiece was a proposal for a united League of Nations that would bring quarreling states to the negotiating table instead of the battlefield. Wilson's European allies, however, showed much greater enthusiasm for the plan than his fellow citizens back home. The Senate, perceiving the organization as a potential threat to national sovereignty, refused to ratify the treaty that would have brought the United States into the league. Undeterred, the president set off on a grueling tour around the country, in search of popular support for the league. But he met with scant sympathy from an increasingly isolationist electorate. His hopes shattered and his health failing, he was forced to return to Washington, where he suffered a massive stroke.

The fact was that Americans wanted little to do with European politics. If Communist revolution could happen in Moscow, why not in Manhattan or Minneapolis? By 1919, citizens of conservative bent were convinced that their way of life was under threat. Their paranoia was fueled by an epidemic of parcel bombs, sent anonymously to prominent politicians, government officials, and public figures such as John D. Rockefeller and J. P. Morgan. Public opinion blamed foreign agitators who arrived with dangerous ideas in their battered suitcases; pressure mounted for the deportation of potentially subversive foreigners. Right-wing extremists took matters into their own hands, forming vigilante groups and lynch mobs against known, or rumored, socialists. In the South, members of a secret society known as the Ku Klux Klan hid themselves beneath white robes and hoods, and rode out to torment—

or murder—blacks, Jews, Catholics, and those whose politics they branded "Red."

Bigotry and paranoia, however, knew no geographical limits. In 1920, in the industrial town of South Braintree, Massachusetts, a messenger carrying the payroll for a local firm was robbed and murdered. Two Italian immigrants, Nicola Sacco and Bartolomeo Vanzetti, were charged with the crime. Sacco, a shoemaker, and Vanzetti, who sold fish from a cart, made no secret of their interest in anarchist ideas; the authorities opined that anyone capable of subscribing to such a dangerous philosophy was equally capable of murder in cold blood. Only the slenderest circumstantial evidence linked the pair to the shooting, but they were found guilty and—despite massive public protests—were executed in 1927.

In the presidential election of 1920, Republican candidate Warren G. Harding struck a chord with many voters when he campaigned with the slogan Return to Normalcy. It was a message that the electorate longed to hear, yet once they had voted him into office, Americans found themselves entering a decade that was anything but normal. The aptly named Roaring Twenties were about to begin.

Collectively, the people of the United States were richer than ever before. Between 1914 and 1920, the country's wealth had increased 250 percent. The urban poor and the farmers of the hard-pressed southern states had little share in the bonanza, but many Americans now possessed an unprecedented amount of money to spend. And spend it they did: on tickets to the movie houses that now provided the nation's favorite form of entertainment, on the radio sets and gramophones that could bring a dance band into every living room, on the automobiles that Henry Ford's mass-production methods had made accessible even to the moderately well-to-do.

The prosperous middle classes could afford to send their sons—and, increasingly, their daughters—to college. The most affluent expanded their horizons even farther, by trips to Europe for the appreciation of high culture. Once there, in the art galleries and the ateliers of Paris, young Americans would discover new ways to view the world—modern painting and sculpture that overturned all the conventions of classical art, and new kinds of poetry and fiction in which words were made to work in radically different ways. Some, seduced, would remain in Europe, joining a growing legion of expatriate artists and intellectuals; others would bring the new ideas back home, and gather to fulfill their fantasies of a creative, bohemian life in Greenwich Village—Manhattan's answer to the intellectual hotbed of Paris's Left Bank.

The old certainties seemed to be collapsing. Women, for instance, were emerging from the kitchen. In 1920, after decades of campaigning, the Nineteenth Amendment to the Constitution gave women the right to vote. They cut their hair, raised their hemlines from the ankle to the knee, entered the work force in ever-greater numbers, and began to ask awkward questions about such subjects as the practice of birth control or the necessity for marriage. Nor was sexual politics the only arena where age-old codes and mores were being challenged. Debate grew increasingly heated over the contradictions between biblical fundamentalism and scientific thought. The twenties would see one of the great trials of the age—the so-called Monkey Trial in 1925—over the right of Tennessee science teacher John Scopes to expound the theory of evolution, and the proposition that humankind was descended from the apes, in contravention of a state law against such irreligious education.

The rule of law itself seemed threatened. Only President Harding's death in 1923, his third year in office, prevented him from being engulfed in a vast political scandal

Carroll Dickerson's jazz band sets the tempo for a floor show at Chicago's Old Sunset Café in 1924. The 1920s saw America's youth flocking to nightclubs in black neighborhoods, where they danced to the music of virtuosos such as Duke Ellington and Louis Armstrong. Musical and moral guardians alike were scandalized: Jazz was "merely a raucous and inarticulate shouting" to one music critic; "reason and reflection are lost," complained a New York physician. Such traditionalists saw jazz, along with intemperance, as a sign of the new social values that threatened to destroy established authority. But just as Prohibition failed to quench the thirst for alcohol, so disapproval seemed only to fuel the rage for jazz. By the end of the decade, both the new music and the new morals were firmly established.

over the leasing of government-owned oil reserves at Teapot Dome, Wyoming, to a corrupt entrepreneur. Senate investigations revealed that the negotiations for these leases were riddled with bribery and fraud at the highest levels of the federal government: For his part in the proceedings, Harding's secretary of the interior had the dubious distinction of being the first United States Cabinet member to go to prison.

In the aftermath of the decade's most controversial piece of legislation, a sizable proportion of the U.S. population turned into criminals overnight. The Volstead Act, passed in 1920 in response to zealous campaigning by the temperance movement, enforced the Eighteenth Amendment to the Constitution, banning the production and sale of intoxicating beverages. Barred from indulgence in their customary pleasures, hundreds of thousands of previously law-abiding Americans used their ingenuity to find ways around the law. Some struggled to recall the lessons taught in their high-school chemistry classes and experimented with bathtub gin; others joined illicit drinking clubs, the speakeasies, where liquor smuggled in from Canada or Europe was consumed behind guarded doors.

U.S. Treasury Department agents were charged with the near-impossible task of enforcing the legislation. But for every bottle of bootleg whisky or smuggled wine they found, there were untold tens of thousands that slipped through the net. Illegal alcohol was big business, and a new breed of entrepreneurs arose to profit from it. Gangs of racketeers operated in every large town and city, led by such luminaries as Al Capone. Capone and his fellow mobsters did not limit their activities to the production or provision of alcohol: They infiltrated labor unions, bought the cooperation of local politicians, took control of prostitution, extortion, and petty crime. In the efficiency with which they built up their organizations, and the ruthlessness with which they pursued their ends, these underworld barons followed precedents established by the great industrialists of the previous generation. Yet, unlike the men behind the trusts, these new entrepreneurs were not content with merely forcing competitors out of business. They preferred instead to dispose of opponents in the New Jersey marshes or the Hudson River, with concrete blocks tied to their feet.

The sinister business of the mobs and the raffish glamour of the speakeasies, however, was remote from the lives of most Americans, except as sources of copy for the popular press. In the small towns and suburbs, the roar of the twenties was more like a whisper. Young people might shock their puritanical elders by dancing the Charleston instead of the more decorous fox trot; the corner grocer might abandon his sacks and barrels in favor of a hundred colorful and competing packages and cans; the public library's shelves might display daring bestsellers by F. Scott Fitzgerald and Ernest Hemingway—but life and the earning of a living went on much as before, even if the material rewards were higher. In the eyes of many citizens, the "normalcy" promised by the late President Harding had finally arrived.

But the lull would be short-lived. The national economy was overheating, and by 1929, it would collapse with a massive crash. Within a few years, nearly 25 percent of Americans would be unemployed. Millions would lose their savings as banks failed and Wall Street stocks plummeted, and millions would lose their homes as mortgages were foreclosed. Nor would the inhabitants of the United States be the only ones to suffer. When the American economy fell apart, the international marketplace reeled from the impact. The ensuing Great Depression of the 1930s was, ironically, proof positive of the nation's new position as a global power: When chill winds blew through the United States, the whole world shivered in the draft.

In 1910, the respectable retirement community of Hollywood, California, saw the arrival of a group of boisterous people it disdainfully nicknamed Movies, from their trade of making motion pictures. Within four years, however, the word "movie" referred not to the newcomers, but to the 4.9 million feet of developed film they produced each year. By 1914, Hollywood was on the road to becoming the center of America's multimillion-dollar film industry. Its movies would provide a prime form of escape in the war years to come.

It was not just California's climate (350 days of sunshine a year guaranteed by the Los Angeles Chamber of Commerce) that drew the filmmakers to Hollywood. Chief among Hollywood's attractions was its distance from New York and Thomas Edison's Motion Picture Patents Company. Though not the sole inventor of moving pictures (the Lumière brothers had been showing motion pictures in Paris as early as 1895), Edison and other investors had bought up patents in 1909 to acquire an effective monopoly over American film production. For five cents, audiences could enter a nickelodeon to see one of Edison's silent, ten-minute one-reelers, shot on the rooftops of Chicago and New York City in natural light. In 1909, with nickelodeons drawing an estimated annual attendance of one billion—mostly low-paid immigrants—moviemaking was big business, which the Motion Picture Patents Company protected with lawyers, detectives, and even hired thugs.

Southern California, on the other side of the continent, offered an ideal escape; should the law intervene, movie crews could simply run for the Mexican border. The Hollywood producers used their independence to the full, and in so doing,

changed the nature of film. The Patents Company had tried to maximize profits by keeping costs to a minimum; Hollywood, however, thrived on extravagance. Directors such as D. W. Griffith and Cecil B. De Mille—seen below shooting his *Male and Female* in 1919—made ever-bigger and more-spectacular multireel epics, which played to prosperous middle-class audiences in opulent "picture shows" around the globe. Actors who had been kept anonymous by the cost-conscious Patents Company now reveled in nationwide personality cults. By the time "talkies," with their synchronized soundtracks, arrived in 1928, Hollywood was a household name to the many millions who daily flocked to the world's motion-picture theaters.

...ish hangs her
...shame as an un-
...ther in D. W. Grif-
...y *Down East*
...Gish, a former
...or, maintained
...f innocence and
...to become one of
...screen goddesses.

Mary Pickford sports char-
acteristic ringlets in *Tess
of the Storm Country*
(1922). With her golden
curls and tiny frame, Pickford embodied sentimental
childhood. Even in her
thirties she wore children's
clothes and appeared on
specially enlarged sets.

SWASHBUCKLERS AND LOVERS: ESCAPE INTO ROMANCE

Rudolph Valentino exercises his irresistible magnetism in *The Sheik* (1921). Women adored Valentino, the archetypal romantic hero; at the height of his fame, he received nine sacks of fan mail per day.

For many viewers, the movies were an escape into a world of romance. Extravagant biblical and historical epics provided a welcome counterpoint to everyday cares; and the public loved the sumptuousness of great costume dramas, such as Douglas Fairbanks's *Robin Hood* and *The Thief of Bagdad,* and Rudolph Valentino's *The Sheik*. To flesh out the fantasy, movie studios vied with one another in creating ever more lavish sets: The set for *Robin Hood* was said to cover almost ten acres. The salaries that accompanied these costly productions—by 1918, top box-office stars like Mary Pickford might earn more than one million dollars a year—only served to contribute to America's romantic visions of Hollywood.

Moviegoers followed the offscreen lives of their idols as closely as they did their films and avidly read about their wealth and luxurious lifestyles in a growing range of fan magazines. After the marriage of Douglas Fairbanks and Mary Pickford in 1920, their European honeymoon tour became a regal progress—300,000 people turned out to welcome them in Moscow alone. In the United States, Rudolph Valentino's death in 1926 inspired several suicides, his funeral mass hysteria.

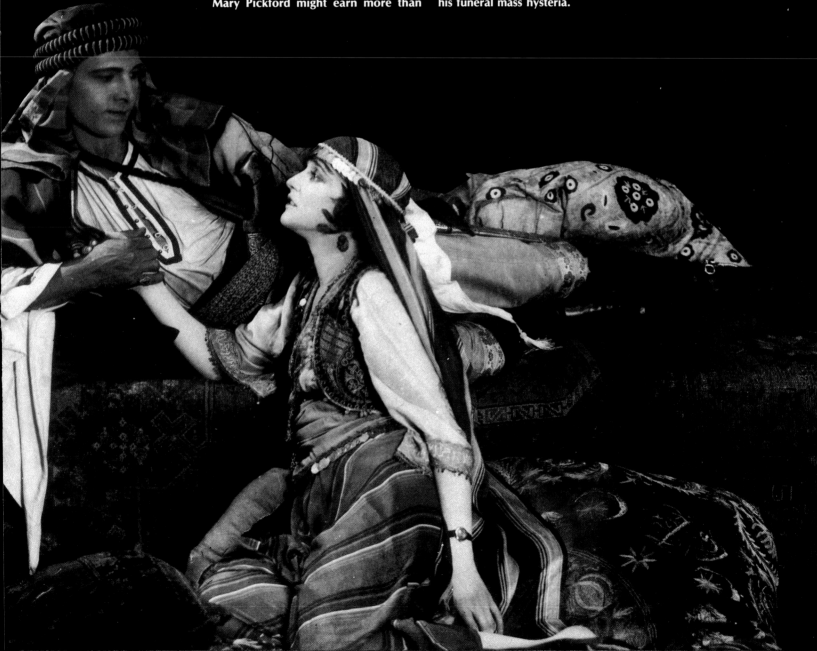

In the saddle for *Our Hospitality* (1923), Buster Keaton maintains an un-smiling expression. Master of the visual gag, Keaton was a versatile performer, taking on many different roles and displaying real genius as a director.

The mild-mannered college boy in trouble once more, Harold Lloyd performs a vertiginous stunt in *Safety Last* (1923). Lloyd resented his stereotyping as a stunt comedian but, despite having lost the use of his right hand, gained great fame for his death-defying escapades.

Truncheons at the ready, the Keystone Kops race to another law-enforcement disaster. In hundreds of short, fast-moving comedies, the Kops undermined authority in all its forms. With tight drilling by creator Mack Sennett in hectic and often dangerous routines, service in the

STUNTS AND SLAPSTICK: THE SILENT COMEDIES

Silent films naturally excelled in visual slapstick comedy. Hollywood actors such as Charlie Chaplin, Buster Keaton, and Harold Lloyd adapted the traditional components of vaudeville and farce to the new conditions of motion pictures. Many early comedies developed no real story line, tending to be merely strings of riotous stunts and sight gags delivered at dizzying speed. These were, nevertheless, carefully planned and executed, particularly under the meticulous supervision of Mack Sennett at his Keystone studios.

The silent comedies were an immediate international success, especially in Europe during the gloomy years of the Great War. In spite of the light relief they provided, however, such movies could have their more serious side. Chaplin in particular frequently combined humor with pathos and social criticism.

A starving Charlie Chaplin dines on his shoe in *The Gold Rush* (1925). The English-born Chaplin often addressed serious social issues in his films; nevertheless, in the role of a tramp—hapless, melancholy, and yet absurdly dignified—he never failed to amuse his audience.

From the outset, moviemakers realized the box-office appeal of sex and violence, and soon began to draw on real-life situations. Against a background of prohibition gangsters, jazz music, and open sex, Hollywood's directors gladly enlarged upon the popular notion of modern life as being unspeakably—but watchably—decadent.

Moralists were soon inveighing against improprieties, both on- and offscreen. In 1921, when the comic star Roscoe "Fatty" Arbuckle was charged with manslaughter in the death of a young woman at a twenty-four-hour party, Hollywood was forced to take preemptive action. The following year, the producers appointed the postmaster general, Will H. Hays, as censor.

Still, the moviemakers soon found ways of circumventing the Hays Office. Sex, violence, and crime were paraded across the screen to be legitimized, belatedly, by final scenes of reform or punishment. And biblical epics, to which no moralist could possibly object, provided magnificent cover.

Lon Chaney plays a crippled gangster in *The Penalty* (1920). Called the Man of a Thousand Faces, Chaney was famous for his macabre disguises.

Theda Bara exudes malevolent sexuality in *Cleopatra* (1917). With the help of a spurious Arab name and lineage, Theodosia Goodman came to represent the seductive vamp to millions of moviegoers.

A Roman orgy scene is used to reflect modern decadence in Cecil B. De Mille's *Manslaughter* (1922). De Mille, most famous for his Old Testament epics, reveled in the camouflaging of titillating material in historical or biblical contexts.

THE FRONTIER LEGEND

Throughout the United States and Europe, touring shows had popularized the idea of the Wild West as entertainment long before the days of film. Movie Westerns were an instant success, starting with D. W. Griffith's *The Great Train Robbery* (1903)—the first narrative film ever made—and the move to Hollywood, close to spectacular desert landscapes, served only to accelerate their production.

The essential characteristics of the Western were quickly established. The rootless, solitary hero found plenty of scope for action in the tribulations of young frontier communities striving for law and order. Westerns thus evoked patriotic myths of American nationhood and history, and the taming of the wilderness—but their appeal was worldwide.

Townsman tussles with cowboy in William S. Hart's *Tumbleweeds* (1925). Hart's last film, which combined romanticism with gritty realism, proved highly influential for later directors.

Wagons ford a river in James Cruze's *The Covered Wagon* (1923). Himself the survivor of a wagon-train trek, Cruze researched his masterpiece in unprecedented detail, reconstructing costumes and equipment with scrupulous authenticity. The film's unsensational documentary quality won new respect for the Western.

William S. Hart leads the fight for justice in *The Gun Fighter* (1917). Hart, a former Shakespearean actor, brought a new seriousness and realism to the Western, as both actor and director.

	1900-1905	**1905-1910**	**1910-1915**

THE MIDDLE EAST

1905-1910
The Young Turks seize power in Istanbul and turn the Ottoman Empire into a constitutional monarchy (1908).

The Ottoman sultan Abdul Hamid is deposed (1909).

1910-1915
Italy seizes Libya, Rhodes, and the Dodecanese Islands from the Ottomans (1912).

The Ottoman Empire enters the Great War on the side of Germany (1914).

EUROPE

1900-1905
King Humbert of Italy is assassinated by an anarchist (1900).

Britain's Queen Victoria dies, to be succeeded by her son, Edward VII (1901).

The Triple Alliance between Germany, Austria-Hungary, and Italy is renewed (1902).

1905-1910
The Triple Entente between Britain, France, and Russia is signed (1907).

Austria-Hungary annexes the Ottoman province of Bosnia-Herzegovina. Bulgaria simultaneously declares its independence from the Ottoman Empire (1908).

1910-1915
George V succeeds as king of England (1910).

Bulgaria, Greece, Serbia, and Montenegro defeat the Ottomans in the First Balkan War (1912).

Serbia, Greece, and Rumania ally against Bulgaria in the Second Balkan War, allowing the Ottomans to regain territory in Europe (1913).

Archduke Francis Ferdinand of Austria-Hungary is assassinated at Sarajevo (1914).

Austria declares war on Serbia, and Europe enters general conflict (1914).

RUSSIA

1900-1905
The supposed mystic Rasputin arrives in the Russian capital of Saint Petersburg and gains entry into court circles (1900).

V. I. Lenin forms the Bolshevik party (1901).

Russia goes to war with Japan (1904).

1905-1910
Soldiers fire on a peaceful demonstration, and the country rises in revolution. Strikes cripple industry until Czar Nicholas II issues the October Manifesto, creating an elected assembly (1905).

Russia concedes defeat in the Russo-Japanese War (1905).

1910-1915
Germany declares war on Russia at the start of the world war (1914).

German forces inflict a heavy defeat on the Russian army at the Battle of Tannenberg (1914).

THE FAR EAST

1900-1905
The Boxer Rebellion, aiming to rid China of foreigners, is crushed by European and Japanese troops (1900).

Russia occupies the Chinese province of Manchuria (1900).

The Anglo-Japanese alliance is signed, assuring each party of mutual support in the event of war (1902).

Russia and Japan go to war over Manchuria (1904).

1905-1910
Japan decimates Russia's navy at the Battle of Tsushima to emerge as the victor in the war. Peace comes with the Treaty of Portsmouth (1905).

1910-1915
Japan annexes Korea (1910).

The Chinese Republic is established after the child emperor Pu Yi is deposed (1911).

Japan's Meiji emperor dies (1912).

Japan enters the Great War as an ally of Britain (1914).

THE UNITED STATES

1900-1905
President McKinley is assassinated by an anarchist, and Theodore Roosevelt is sworn in as his successor (1901).

Wilbur and Orville Wright make the first manned, powered flight in an airplane (1903).

1905-1910
An earthquake followed by a catastrophic fire devastates San Francisco (1906).

William Howard Taft becomes president (1909).

1910-1915
Ford Motor Company begins assembly-line production (1910).

Movie producers move to Hollywood from the East Coast (1910).

The world's largest ocean liner, the *Titanic*, hits an iceberg off the North American coast on its maiden voyage and 1,513 passengers are drowned (1912).

Woodrow Wilson becomes president (1913).

The Panama Canal is completed (1914).

TimeFrame AD 1900-1925